The

Last Day
of
Regret

Matthew J. Diaz

WESTBOW
PRESS®
A DIVISION OF THOMAS NELSON
& ZONDERVAN

WestBow Press books may be ordered through booksellers or by contacting:

WestBow Press
A Division of Thomas Nelson & Zondervan
1663 Liberty Drive
Bloomington, IN 47403
www.westbowpress.com
1 (866) 928-1240

Cover Art: Carissa Eich
Editor: Alicia Wall

ISBN: 978-1-9736-5740-8 (sc)
ISBN: 978-1-9736-5742-2 (hc)
ISBN: 978-1-9736-5741-5 (e)

Library of Congress Control Number: 2019903307

Print information available on the last page.

WestBow Press rev. date: 3/28/2019

Acknowledgments

I have written this book for my stepdad, although I do not know if he will ever have the strength to read it. I know he wanted me to record his daughter's legacy through my eyes because he trusted me to share my sister's story. God gave me a yearning to put on paper the vision He gave me a month after my sister passed away. I simply needed the past four years to process it.

I dedicate this book to my mom and my stepdad, who have been humbled by death and have shown me how to live even when the worst pain imaginable occurs. Death shows no favoritism or prejudice, and it waits for no one. From the depths of my soul, my voice cries out, "Our time is short, beloved. Do you know the one who can conquer this death?" Whether you have an answer to that question or not, this story is for you.

Thank you to my wife, Katie. You have taken this lowly man and shown me love and value. You have revealed to me how Jesus sees me—forgiven and free. I choose no other person but you to experience life with. Hannah loved you, loved me, and loved our children. Indeed, our family is a testimony to Hannah's life. Thank you for mothering our four children. We see your constant sacrifice for all of us, for the quintessence of our family is Christ shining so brightly in you.

To my surviving siblings, our deepest pain of losing a sibling presents to us a great journey we must travel. You are here for a reason; you have a purpose, and you are fearfully and wonderfully made. We all have grieved in our own way, and I pray you will find some healing of this wound that we share by revisiting our time together that difficult week and in some of the stories of our childhood. Forgive me if I fail to mention a detail or two, but the heart of what I want to capture is there.

I have always looked up to you as my guardians. One of you threw punches for me when other kids would make fun of my hearing impairment. The other would allow me to wake you up to comfort me when I had a nightmare. You would make a bed of blankets on the ground so I wasn't alone on my part of the bunk beds. Lastly, one of you walked me through my eighth-grade registration day so I was spared the middle-school turmoil of parental embarrassment—no offense, Mom.

You also showed me the ropes of college my first semester. We took an acting class together, and as you always have, you helped me at the next stage of my life. All three of you have protected me, and I need you to know that a major reason I look back on my life and love my upbringing is because of you. I can't imagine it any other way. In all the bad and the good, I'm grateful for our friendship and the genuine love we share for each other as adults now raising children of our own.

A special thanks to Carissa Eich, who illustrated the cover of this book. Given pictures of Hannah's tattoos, Carissa dreamed up something singularly meaningful, just as I asked. With much prayer and thought, she brought to life a unique and precious piece of art for which I am forever grateful. Thank you to Alicia Wall as well for coaching me through this writing process and helping me hone my skills as an author. Thank you to everyone at Northwest Christian School, especially Geoff Brown who constantly encouraged me to write down this story and has allowed it to be stitched into the fabric of our community. Thank you Cornerstone Church, @cornerstonechandler, for your part in Hannah's story.

In truth and love,
Matthew J. Diaz
September 1, 2018

But your dead will live, LORD;
their bodies will rise—
let those who dwell in the dust
wake up and shout for joy—
your dew is like the dew of the morning;
the earth will give birth to her dead.
—Isaiah 26:19

Contents

Introduction

This isn't just my sister's story; it is very much my story and my perspective on our lives. The book begins with an introduction to Hannah and the tumultuous relationship we shared. Next, I go back to the point where our relationship went awry and recount the events leading up to her passing. Along the way, I share lessons I have learned as I reflect on the journey God brought me on. My hope is that the backstory regarding this journey will effectively reveal the weight of her death when it occurred, because the only way to discuss Hannah and give her story the justice it deserves is to walk you through the years that led up to her death.

As for her untimely departure, I revisit the details of Hannah's death—and the week between her death and funeral—so that you, my fellow sojourner, might feel the weight of the burden I carried. If you have never experienced a loss, this will shed some light in the hope that you will be able to get a glimpse of the reality of those who have. Many details about death are unknown until you lose someone. Like planning a wedding, planning a funeral and laying to rest someone who has died is emotionally taxing to say the least.

As I discuss my relationship with Hannah, I also share the grim details of the process of how we care for our loved ones in death. If you have lost someone, please make sure you are in a healthy place to reopen the wound or scar you carry, and allow God to heal you as you read what may seem very familiar to you. Don't worry; I will leave you with hope, for it's what keeps me moving forward. It is a hope that no matter how we feel today, the best days of our lives are still ahead of us.

Over the years, I have shared different aspects of the life of my sister Hannah with hundreds of high school students. I've shared her pain of cutting, suicidal thoughts, and drug use, and her path of turning back to God. I've shared my own experience of losing a sibling, especially recognizing that I wasn't always the best sibling to her once we became adults. I've shared about her psychological disorder and the challenges that a Borderline Personality Disorder (BPD) presents. God has shown me clearly that this story isn't just for me but for everyone who has asked the question, "Why does God allow me to suffer?"

We all suffer. Sometimes we cause our own suffering, and sometimes we cause others to suffer. It is intertwined within our fallen human condition to constantly struggle with how much suffering we will perpetuate on any given day with any given choice. Somewhere in my story and relationship with my sister, I had hardened my heart toward her. I caused Hannah pain, and I held grudges and was unforgiving.

The day Hannah died, my heart of stone just disappeared. There was no one to be hard-hearted toward, for she was gone. This experience allowed me to see, through God's eyes, the path I'd traveled over the preceding decade. It is this decade I share with you: where Hannah and I started, where our stories diverged, where they clashed together, and how I slowly healed.

Several months drifted by after Hannah died before I visited Hannah's therapist, who had made herself available for counseling because she was in a unique position to help me understand Hannah and her borderline personality traits. What the therapist told me that day removed my guilt, and I drove home with my burden lifted. She shared that Hannah loved me and, more than that, wanted to defend me at all costs. Hannah saw me as someone who needed her protection; she saw me as someone deserving her time and energy to fight for even when I did not reciprocate. Hannah had not given up on me. In that moment, I let go of my shame and guilt. I was free to love as Hannah loved: unconditionally.

Prologue

If I am honest, if I do not write these events down, I will forget them, and I never want to forget them. How else could I recollect an entire life's events of another person in something as small as a book? Surely the actual transcript of the life of my sister Hannah would generate volumes upon volumes. It would be enough to warrant her own section in the library.

My beloved sister's life would be in the adult nonfiction section, with each book labeled *H5* along the spine: *H* for Hannah (it should be listed by her last name, *Zeller*, but she absolutely hated always being last on the school rosters for everything) and *5* for being the fifth child in our family, the youngest. This section would be easy to spot; it would stand out among the rest because of all the colors, patterns, and crafts protruding from the stacks. The shelves would be lined with markings of a sharpie showing Hannah's various doodles and drawings made throughout her life as well as every tattoo she had accumulated. Every book would have a different penguin scribbled on its inside cover, with no two looking the same, because Hannah owned a multitude of stuffed toy penguins of various shapes, sizes, and colors.

Each book would be covered with an eclectic assortment of colors and styles of duct tape to protect the contents, and the pages would be bright pink, since Hannah managed to convince our parents to paint her bedroom from top to bottom in what looked like the medicine you hate to drink for an upset stomach. The cover of Hannah's last book would be carefully crafted out of wood but lined with light blue duct tape, with pictures of small black-and-white cartoon-shaped penguins in a pattern across every inch of the tape. There would be signatures on the cover from all sorts of family and friends who had been part of the various stories throughout Hannah's life. It's as if this book cover were a cast for a broken arm that she would be removing someday. This last book would best represent Hannah and would stand out the most, simply due to its unique design. You can, in fact, judge *this* book by its cover.

Unfortunately for us, Hannah's story was cut short. The writing of her life suddenly stopped between the hours of eight-thirty and ten on one frightful Friday morning. We will never know how large these unwritten books would have been if the writing had continued until a more natural time in life took Hannah away.

If we were to read the ten books representing the previous decade of Hannah's life, we would find countless places where the words statistically should have stopped. With all the chances she took— teetering between life and death both for recreation and in depression— Hannah played Russian roulette plenty of times. However, she managed to keep writing through the blood, sweat, and tears.

There are moments of suffering in the life of my sister Hannah, and it is the last ten books that contained the most pain—pain that defined and marked her. Those nights of drinking, drugs, sex, overeating, cutting, and numbing the ever-deepening sadness in her heart would be inscribed in these darker books. The nights where Hannah felt so hopeless and desperate for love and forgiveness but also so shameful and alone would not be missed. Hannah carried this regret, and the vicious cycle of addiction was her way of escaping the pain. Regret about having gone down that road in the first place would keep her there. Who would be able to stomach this dark journey of Hannah's? Perhaps only those who have been there themselves, who understand the world that she lived in. In her early years, Hannah's world was full of light and laughter, but the latter section of her life became a shadow of what those innocent years of her life once were.

Every great story has a period of time when the hero is lost, where events seem hopeless, and where the ending seems inevitably dreadful and miserable. Hannah's journey is no different. Hannah began her life courageously, but at some point, she lost her way, and her life filled with sorrow. However, even though there was a decade of pain, it is in Hannah's last book—the one that got cut short, the one with the beautiful blue duct tape with penguins and signatures from old and new friends—that she overcame the hero's trial. This is how we know that it is okay that the writing came to an end. Hannah had finally fought through the darkness. Her struggles did not disappear in her life; temptation can still lurk within the far crevices of our mind. However, regret no longer held Hannah down—the regret that had kept her from the purposeful life that is possible for us all.

All great endings seem to come quickly and, in fact, only last a fraction of the entirety of the story. This is how it was with Hannah's life journey. Of her twenty-four years of life, it is the end that defined her, redeemed her, and made her passing inexplicably hopeful. Her surviving family members visit this particular volume of Hannah's life often and reflect on how the impact of this tragedy changed their lives forever. Even though she laid her pen down, all stories deserve an epilogue, an explanation of the impact of the written events from years later. The only way to reconcile the pain in Hannah's life would be to give the right amount of attention to it, mixed in with the final events that came with her passing.

The irony of it all is that Hannah lived the last decade of her life with regret, and ironically, it is regret that I feel when I think of my relationship with her. This story of Hannah has left an indelible mark on my life. However, Hannah's death, and the pain that she carried, should not be her legacy. One cannot change the past, so stewing over it with regret, wishing one could fix it, does not aid one's journey toward healing. Hannah's darkest moments need to be redeemed by showing the impact her passing has had in the weeks, months, and years that have followed her death.

I am writing this down so that I can remember the reason for the pain, for it is through the pain that Hannah and I shared that I have found peace in our stories. I never want to forget my little sister who loved me so greatly and freely—my sister who had a great desire to defend me and protect me, who taught me how to care and how to be an older sibling. Hannah gave me a vision of what I want for my own children.

Hannah's life has deeply and forever elevated my life. I pray others find the same purpose and hope I have in telling the story of my sister: our tumultuous relationship, the regret I have carried, and how I am learning to still move forward and allow God to slowly carry the pain with and for me.

That's the confusing thing about pain: we want it to stop immediately. It's like a bee sting, a paper cut, or stubbed toe. Our reaction is to shake our appendage violently, hoping for the pain to subside. When the pain lasts longer than what seems appropriate for the stinger to be removed, the cut to be bandaged, or the toe to stop throbbing, we fear something more extensive has occurred. We equate the length of time we experience pain with the size of damage that has occurred.

We bring the same assumptions to our heart. When our heart hurts longer than what we perceive to be an adequate amount of time, our mind moves toward greater depths of hurt. We pray and ask God to remove the sting of death quickly or to bandage the cut of a broken relationship and apply lidocaine liberally. After we have cursed the sky at the inconvenience of tragedy, we pray that the pain will stop. When the pain continues, we wonder what greater problem lies within or start to doubt God's existence. If God were real, wouldn't He take our pain right here and right now? Why didn't He remove my sister's pain when she was a fourteen-year-old girl who had lost her sense of self-worth and would rather entertain suicide as a common thought?

Time is relative, Albert Einstein theorized. "Put your hand on a hot stove for a minute, and it seems like an hour. Sit with a pretty girl for an hour, and it seems like a minute. That's relativity." Our minute of pain appears to be lasting for an eternity. In the grand spectrum of eternity, our pain seems not to be too long of a time to an infinite God. I have come to believe He does not equate the length of time to the depth of the wound. When He heals us, it might seem slow to us, but if time is relative, His pace of healing is perfect.

Would we wish a careless surgeon to quickly suture and cauterize a wound after he had recklessly removed only a few cancerous cells, only to find out months down the road he missed some? Allowing God to heal us, and allowing Him the time necessary to do so, is completely relative. Perhaps this is why the greatest mark of a believer is perseverance, because it is the soul who has fully embraced the truth that God's timing is not our own who can stay the course. God will heal my heart and remove my pain in the right amount of time, as He did heal my sister.

My healing began in an unexpected way and at an unexpected time—or I should say, an unexpected moment in time. From the outside, Hannah's death appeared hopeless and meaningless. People tried to say the right things to make me feel better about the situation, but for a person grieving, it feels all in vain. Before we can draw any significant conclusions about Hannah's death, it would be beneficial to follow her life's journey long before the events that transpired on the day she died and in the week that followed. This is Hannah's redeeming story, all the pain and brokenness captured in a few words to hopefully provide validation for you, my dear reader—validation, perspective, and an adequate response to the regret left by the reality of death, pain, and sorrow.

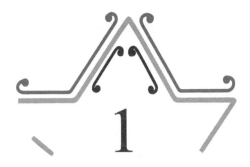

1

The Halloween Debacle

"Hannah wants to make plans for Halloween," my mom was explaining to me over the phone.

"I can't make plans based off of what she wants. I have two boys to think about," I argued back.

"All your sister wants to do is to go trick-or-treating, and she thought it would be fun to go with you around your apartment complex—she says you get the best candy there—and then for you all to go to the carnival at her church where she is volunteering," she explained.

My mom was trying to play peacemaker between my sister and me. We were all living in a large metropolitan area but were technically in two separate cities. My wife, three children, and I were living in an apartment about forty-five minutes away. I had just left—or been asked to leave—a job I had invested a lot of time, energy, and money in while we were pregnant with our third child. That child would come a month early, a baby girl weighing just three pounds and eleven ounces, quickly after our move to the apartment.

Hannah and I had been drifting apart for years. I was twenty-nine, and she was twenty-four. Our communication had regressed backward in time to when we were children fighting over the best spot on the couch to watch TV. I would often be confrontive with her; I had become not so gentle with my words. I had decided that I would either not talk to her at all or be blunt if I needed something. Not talking was easy; trying not to be blunt with my fully grown adult sister was difficult. So I would opt not to talk. The other option was to have my wife talk to Hannah, which she did a lot because they had become close over the years.

My wife has a way with people that makes you feel good about yourself just by having her listen and be engaged and respond with joy, interest, and enthusiasm. Hannah needed that, and I had lost the ability to communicate in that way with her. I was in the most difficult season of my life, and the last person I would consider adjusting plans for was my sister. I had learned years ago that Hannah always wanted more, always took, and it had become draining. I drew a line of how far I was willing to go to accommodate her. Hannah was an adult, and she needed to grow up a little.

I thought to myself three things: one, Hannah was already heavy enough and didn't need more candy; two, she was twenty-four and didn't need to be trick-or-treating in the first place or using my kids to do so; and three, why would I want to go trick-or-treating *and* go to the church carnival on a school night with my two- and seven-year-old rambunctious boys (who would be asking me every second if they could eat the candy) while carrying around a seven-week-old preemie baby who only had energy to eat and sleep? Eating and sleeping were, by the way, two things she prevented *us* from doing. Our colicky little bundle of joy needed to be awakened every three hours to eat until she reached a normal gestation weight. That was a recipe for exhaustion for my wife and I, and it weighed heavily on my decision about plans for Halloween: what was the minimum I could do so my boys were content and I'd exerted the least amount of energy possible, because that is what both my wife and I were low on?

Did my sister Hannah give any thought to my feelings or how difficult my life had been over the past several months? Our baby had to be delivered by C-section because my wife was showing early signs of preeclampsia. Because our tiny newborn weighed only three pounds eleven ounces, she remained in the hospital for two weeks. On top of that, I was working a dead-end job that I had to drive forty-five minutes to each way, through the desert, on the most dangerous road in the state. I had left my career as a youth pastor in search of an organization that was bigger, better, and would provide me with my next step in gaining more experience. I obviously had not found that bigger and better; instead, I was working as a glorified tutor in a computer lab for high school dropouts or kids who did not fit into the high school setting and just wanted to get their coursework out of the way. Not having found what I wanted in ministry, I fell back into teaching, which was what I'd studied for in college. However, my first job offer was at a charter school that only offered a computer lab position.

The ironic thing was that I was neither a pastor nor a teacher. None of the things I had been trained to do were involved in this job. I had learned from my stepdad that you take any job that is offered; you can't be picky when it comes to experience and having a source of income. With four people to take care of, it was not a time for me to be fickle with job offers. I just needed to take it, accept the responsibility to take care of my family, and pray that God would honor my willingness to take a lower-paying position to see to our immediate needs.

"Mom, I don't have time to cater to what Hannah wants. Tell her we will just meet her at the carnival," I explained with my manipulative logic so as not to have her come to the apartment and use my boys as patsies. Katie did not mind staying home with our baby girl, and I hoped that both of them could get some rest. I decided to suck it up and let the kids ride some rides, get some candy for an hour, and call it a night.

Before my mom asked, I told her that we were going to just trick-or-treat around the complex ourselves. I was unwilling to do both things with Hannah. I thought that what she really wanted was for us to see her in her element at a church she had been involved in for a little over a year and where she had started volunteering in the children's ministry. I had not considered her needs in a while, and I thought it would be an easy gesture to bring the boys to see her at the carnival.

Hannah could never talk to me herself, so all verbal transactions were through my mom. Granted, I had given her reason to consider me unapproachable. She avoided conflict, and several years back, I made the decision that avoiding her or confronting her at every angle would be the only way to survive my time around her. If I know there is a problem, my way of fixing it is to deal with it head on, using my bluntness. After that stopped working through many shed tears, my mom eventually became the filter for our communication.

I felt that Mom was just enabling Hannah to not deal with her own problems, but I was not going to create conflict with my mom. I needed my mom too much to break off that relationship. I didn't think I needed a relationship with Hannah at all. But if I neglected Hannah, my mom would be hurt, so I felt like the only way to keep my mom's and my relationship in tact would be to accept Hannah on a surface level and not engage in much more.

I was either verbally directing lines of questions and assaults, building defensive emotional barriers, or being completely silent. My eye contact was minimal; I would just act busy around my sister. It's easy to ignore people when there are lots of things to do. Our visits would be just short enough that I could go through my to-do list and manage not to go deeper than a casual hello and hug goodbye. I would hide behind my wife, allowing Katie to be conversational and for her friendship with Hannah to take the place of my own. Katie became the friend I used to be to Hannah but felt I could no longer be. I could not be Hannah's friend without feeling used, either for my stuff or for her to get something from me.

Some people are givers, and some are takers. My sister was a taker, and my solution was to stop giving. It was Hannah's world, and the rest of us were just living in it. Hannah had my mom and stepdad wrapped around her finger and at her beck and call. Ever since they left our hometown—just the three of them when Hannah was sixteen—she had been an only child. The older four of us had grown up and were on our own, but Hannah still had her teenage years left at that point.

I never really got over the feeling of abandonment when my

mom, stepdad, and Hannah moved to Colorado. I was mad that the reason they moved was for Hannah to start over in a new place. I was jealous that Hannah took all their time and energy. At every wedding, graduation, or big event, Hannah would find a way to bring everything back to herself—or at least take my stepdad away from the event at hand so she could have her timely migraine attended to.

I don't remember when I first started having these brash, judgmental thoughts and observations. Looking back, my reasoning was that I expected Hannah to grow up and be an adult like the rest of us. If she would naturally grow out of her teenage years and become an independent adult, then I could respect her. Hannah would tell me that she felt like I didn't treat her like an adult, and the irony was that I didn't think she *was* an adult. How could I tell Hannah that her assessment was true?

During the year prior to the Halloween debacle, I didn't see that she had grown up, taken responsibility for her life, and stopped relying on mom and dad to support her. I would shrug her off and think that it wasn't true. I treated her like my older siblings treated me at her age. My twisted form of measurement was an eye for an eye, but it was not my eye for hers. It was that my older siblings figuratively took my eye at some point growing up, so I would take one from Hannah. I used to have compassion for her, but whenever it was that I decided she should be an adult, I defaulted to following the letter of the law: "But if there is serious injury, you are to take life for life, eye for eye, tooth for tooth, hand for hand, foot for foot" (Exodus 21:23–24).

The conversation about Halloween ended for a few days, until my mom decided to give it another go. I assumed that was after she talked it over with Hannah—because, of course, Hannah couldn't talk to me herself.

"I don't think Hannah really cares about the carnival. She just thought that would be fun for you. She really just wants to go trick-or-treating with all of you," my mom said in a desperate tone.

"Okay, fine, she can come, but we don't have time for the carnival if that's what she really wants."

It was all about free candy for Hannah—the only night she didn't have to pay for the candy that she hid in her room and yet left the wrappers for anyone to find. When she said she wanted to spend time with my boys but at the same time said she can score the most candy if she comes along, a red flag waved around in my head that I was being used. What adult goes trick-or-treating, still trying to fill a pillowcase with free candy? That was my sister's goal, and if that was how she wanted to present herself, then I could not stop her, though I did try.

This whole conversation had started over the misunderstanding that Hannah was demanding that we do everything she planned, regardless of my opinion. I had typically, and often, seen Hannah in a selfish light over the past six years. She'd called me out on my treatment of her on more than one occasion.

"You have changed. Why can't it be the way it used to be?" she would ask. I never had a clear answer; I simply would use my marriage as an excuse and say I didn't have the emotional energy to care for my young family and for her. Hannah wanted me to cater to her as I used to, when I would take her to the movies or drive several hours to a concert we both enjoyed, but I couldn't anymore. I used to have this place in my heart reserved just for her, where I cared deeply for her well-being and emotional state, but that place had been rented out to time and space ever since the move to Colorado had distanced us.

It was during her time in Colorado that I grew up, and I expected that she'd grow up within the same time frame as I did. It had been eight years from the time Hannah, my mom, and my stepdad had moved away to Colorado, to the Halloween incident before Hannah's passing. As I have mentioned, she was twenty-four and I was twenty-nine, so surely all of life's rules and consequences should be equally applied to the both of us. When I was twenty-four, I was pursuing my wife, who had a two-year-old son at the time. I wanted Hannah to see that she was a little behind overall in the growing-up thing. In reality, she was well aware of her shortcomings.

Hannah was not as ignorant as I had assumed, and her accusations of how I felt about her and treated her were all true. I was just too prideful to admit that to her or change. Hannah was heavily dependent on my parents. She was a community college dropout with no job. I guess my view of her showed. I did not realize that my scheme of ignoring her was speaking louder than my actual words. The Halloween plans were just a symptom of a greater problem of how I viewed Hannah: as a self-absorbed, whining, stuck-as-a-teenager hypochondriac.

I was convinced that hypochondria explained Hannah's intense need for attention. Every time there was a diagnosis in our family or extended family of any kind of psychiatric disorder, Hannah mysteriously had it too. In my own dysfunction, I found myself increasingly irritated with Hannah. I was given the diagnosis of obsessive compulsive disorder (OCD) when I was twenty-three, and I had been seeking treatment for it ever since. I was frustrated with Hannah the more she researched the symptoms of OCD to see how my experience related to her. Lo and behold, within several months of my own diagnosis, Hannah proclaimed that she was OCD as well. She would insert into conversations how her OCD told her to do this or that.

When she was a teenager with depression, I had sympathy for her and could empathize, but as we became adults, I found it selfish of her to label herself with these varying disorders. The final proof that she was making everything up was when Katie and I found out, when our son was four, that he had sensory processing disorder. As I could have predicted, all of a sudden, Hannah claimed she was experiencing all the same symptoms as her nephew. I just rolled my eyes at that point. Had she never heard of a self-fulfilling prophecy? Hannah was the walking textbook definition.

Of course, my own diagnosis of Hannah's hypochondria was so much deeper than that. I'd started noticing these interesting behavior patterns years before the Halloween debacle. I noticed something had changed in Hannah, although perhaps it had been there all along. Hannah was diagnosed with Borderline Personality Disorder (BPD) at the age of twenty, but it had been brewing in the back recesses of her mind since she was fourteen. I had great compassion for her when she was first admitted into the behavioral health wing at the hospital, but honestly, after a decade of what I called "crying wolf," I did not care; it just seemed like an excuse for her to act however she wanted.

It wasn't until a year and a half after Hannah's death that I met another person with BPD and was forced to learn exactly what Hannah carried around with her. All the problems I'd experienced with Hannah as she became an adult, and as I became an adult, could be traced back to a lack of understanding about her BPD. I was not too far off with the whole hypochondria guess; she did think she had those disorders, but not for the same reason as a real hypochondriac who has a fear of getting every type of sickness. Hannah was never afraid of her self-diagnosis; she just added it to a list of things that, to her, explained her behavior.

In the years following her death, I was shown that the BPD component that explained her hypochondria was a desperate need for attention and validation. If she saw that any of us was getting attention for a disorder, she needed that attention too. When I felt that everything was about her, once I studied the traits of a person with BPD, I learned it really *was* about her, and that was a major part of the struggle.

After doing some research and having a book recommended to me, *Stop Walking on Eggshells* by Paul T. Mason, MS, I started putting the pieces together of what exactly went wrong in my relationship with Hannah. I often felt that she would create these lose-lose scenarios where no matter what I did, she would come out as the victim and I the antagonist. It turns out that people who have BPD do exactly that. Their deepest insecurities about themselves turn out to be what drive their behavior and create contradictions of how they treat people around them.

Often, people with BPD act out with the people closest to them. At some point in time, I had forgotten how close I was with my younger sister and that our problem stemmed from my not understanding that she treated me the way she did because of how close she felt to me relationally, even compared to our older siblings. The other half of the problem was my lack of empathy, maturity, and humility. If I'd known the things I know now about people with BPD, I would have at least had empathy.

Empathy is what allows us to see other people as we see ourselves. It comes when we think of ourselves less and take a moment to live the life of another person and understand his or her pain and problems. It's been called walking in another person's shoes. My feet were not much bigger than Hannah's, and I could have walked very well in some of the many shoes she collected over the years. I simply chose not to. I had entered my twenties and become an adult, and I expected her to do the same. When she did not match up to my expectations, I judged her for it, although I had set the bar at an unattainable height. The expectation in my mind was simple: "Act like an adult, and I will treat you as an equal." Until she could do so, I kept her at a distance.

Several years after Hannah's passing, one of my older sisters wrote me an email saying that she missed the "kind and understanding Matt Jo. Where is your compassion? Where is my younger brother who is empathetic, kind, and caring?" Hannah was right about me, but it took hearing it a second time from my older sister to register. Hannah saw right through me and knew I was treating her differently, even though I did not want to admit it.

I had started selectively loving the people around me based on whether I felt I could give them that love. I was disconnected from what love truly is; therefore, I only had a limited amount of love to share. My boundaries to keep my own heart safe and secure required that I limit who received love from me. My love was conditional and reserved only for my wife and children. Other than that, I had no time or energy to invest in any other family member. I always thought it was Hannah's problem, but when my older sister confronted me years after Hannah's passing, I realized I was the common denominator in this equation of broken relationships.

Another great regret was learning about Hannah's deepest pain too late—and learning that I was acting out of my own pain. A broken person cannot love a broken person well. I did not see myself as broken.

It's like what Jesus said to the church in Ephesus in Revelation 2:5: "Consider how far you have fallen! Repent and do the things you did at first." I had forgotten that I too had fallen from grace, and it would be a long time before I repented.

It wasn't until after I had gotten married, took on a stepson, and moved to live with my mom, stepdad, and Hannah in Colorado Springs that the division between Hannah and I was made most evident. I had absolutely no compassion for Hannah, and that became clear within the first few weeks of our arrival at the house on Stone Fence Drive. Hannah's brokenness and my brokenness would collide, and the result was silence.

I didn't talk to her, and although she tried to talk to me, I wouldn't keep the conversation going or stick around very long. My heart had grown cold; I thought I was masking it well, but Hannah had great empathy. She knew how I felt without me needing to say anything. Hannah knew she was broken. She just wanted me to understand her, and I didn't. Our time living together in Colorado would end with what I have called the Colorado Confrontation, which has been a major source of regret since her passing.

My time on Stone Fence Drive is a paradox in my life. I wish I had not moved there at all, and yet without it, Hannah's death would not have the distinct impact it has had on my life today. We sometimes wonder if God could possibly pick up the pieces of our failed choices. I often wonder if there is anything I can do to mess up God's will for my life. What if I already have done that? Is there a way to just pack it up and move on and not deal with broken things? Can we just leave them on the side of the road or throw them in the trash and not have them damage us in some way?

God, over a long period of time both before and after Hannah's death, has shown me that the pain is necessary to understand both humanity and, ultimately, God's grace. It's what Jesus did: he became human so that he could empathize with our pain and offer the grace that we could not give ourselves. My relationship with Hannah is both a regret and a necessity to be able to share this story. It is this story that will be used to change lives.

Would I rather have my sister here with me today? Most people would say yes—it is an automatic response. I would say that if the person who was lost was a sort of glue, the type that held things together, then yes, we would always want that person back. However, Hannah was in deep pain; Hannah was suffering in this life, and Hannah was deeply broken. If I am honest with myself, I'm not sure having her back is even something to consider.

On the one hand, we cannot go back and change anything, and yet in the world of hypothetical situations, I do not know all the things God was sparing her from. It appeared in the months leading up to Hannah's death that she was doing much better than the past five or six years. However, there were more than a dozen other times her life could have been taken and yet she lived. There must have been a reason God allowed and accounted for Hannah's departure from this earthly plane in just the way it happened.

I believe she lived no longer and no less than what God intended. I honestly believe her life would have continued to be one of suffering and misery; maybe God in His mercy spared us from something that would have been even more tragic. I do not think it is worth my time imagining what could be worse, but the reality is that it could have been worse, and Hannah's untimely death is something I choose to believe God has used and will use for His good ends.

My relationship with Hannah wasn't always so stressful. We had a whole lifetime before things changed at the house on Stone Fence Drive. There was even a time while Hannah was living at that house that we created amazing and unforgettable memories. At some point along the way, those memories started to fade because they had become painful— for me but probably even more so for Hannah. It's easy to get wrapped up in painful memories, because sometimes the pain in our lives seems stronger than the feelings or memories of times without pain. Pain seems to be an overpowering odor in our minds that no amount of perfume, cologne, or spice can cover. The bad smell is still there and very apparent, but even worse is that the good smell no longer smells good at all. The smell of pain is hard to scrub out of the recesses of our minds.

If the opposite of pain is joy, a person could assume you are either fully in one state or the other. However, there is a third feeling that is an attempt to replace the pain, and that is apathy or numbness. In reality, joy represents just one third of our feelings. The other two, psychologically, are not good to live in because living in pain or apathy does not promote growth, health, positive change, and most importantly, a positive self-image. If you don't view yourself well, you will not perceive others well.

The measure by which you view yourself is usually the measure that you project onto God as well. There is a point in our conversion to our faith in Christ where we must recognize our own shortcomings. We cannot approach God with an attitude that needs nothing, reflecting apathy. What is needed is to bring God our pain, a recognition that our lives are not as they are supposed to be, and an acknowledgement that He alone can fix the problem.

A man who claimed to be this very God walked the earth two thousand years ago and addressed this very problem of pain. He stated, "In this world you will have trouble" (John 16:33). Trouble comes in all forms, and one of the most distinct ways we are emotionally aware of trouble is pain. This God-man finishes the statement by saying, "But take heart! I have overcome the world" (John 16:33). If we live only in pain after we have already acknowledged all that Jesus has done for us, then it seems we are living in the very condition Jesus wanted to free us from. We feel pain but were never meant to carry it on our own.

Hannah knew pain, and it would take me a lot longer to realize how great her pain was and how my own hurt would become a hindrance to her. I changed from a loving brother to a judgmental one, and if I look back and retrace my steps, I eventually recognize what happened. I've heard it said that "Hurting people hurt people." This would be true of my relationship with Hannah. To validate Hannah's pain and recognize where our lives diverged, I must share events well before her tragic death, as well as those surrounding the week leading into it and the day of her funeral. Putting these pieces together has led me to see, finally, what Jesus promised: the part where He says He has "overcome the world." To state it another way, Jesus even overcomes our own self-inflicted wounds.

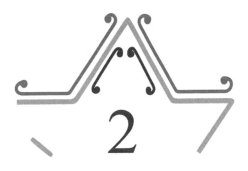

2

About A Boy

I met and married Katie after I graduated from college, but it was a union of more than just two people. Katie had a child from a previous relationship. The interesting part of the story is that I met Kyle first.

When Kyle was nine months old, I was a youth pastor at a church in my hometown, and one of my youth ministry volunteers would babysit for Katie periodically and bring Kyle with her to church. It was a year before I met Katie. At the time, all I knew was that there was a giant man-baby who walked up and down the hallway staring into my office on any given workday. Kyle barely had any hair, and the hair he had was blond to match his fair complexion. He had blueish eyes, a big round head, and the biggest smile on his face, all while wearing a onesie. He was a little big baby.

I'm not sure why Kyle was in his pajamas so often. I think he liked the comfort of them. He wasn't fat; he was just tall with a big head and even bigger eyes. I would look over at him and Kyle would smile, and then he would run away, giggling at his cleverness.

I finally met Katie at one of the church's college-age hangouts when I first started leading the college ministry in addition to the middle school ministry. It was in the woods at someone's house, in a large backyard with a heated pool that had an adjacent spa. During that spring and into the summer season, the college-aged group spent many nights together at that house in the woods. The owners were always away, and they let us use it because we were all good "church" kids. The girls would play board games and the boys would figure out how to either challenge each other's manhood or scare the girls once it was dark.

The boys went to great lengths—literally distance—to sneak around the entire house so that we were not at our original trajectory toward the house. We had the freedom of the woods and the curse of twigs and pine cones that echoed in the dark. The real challenge of our manliness was whether we could quietly circumnavigate the entire perimeter of the house without being noticed. When we reached the secondary objective, we would hear high-pitched screams and laughter from the girls who were waiting in fear and anticipation that we were out there, up to something.

Side note: If a group of friends is ever in a house in the middle of the woods, and there is even one male in the group, be prepared to have a few windows tapped ever so lightly at multiple entry points. All the horror movies that take place at night in the woods use the window-tapping tactic. Don't ever underestimate the fear invoked upon unwitting prey, especially friends.

Almost a year into our marriage I pulled the window-tapping prank when Katie and I lived in our first home, which was in the woods next to the train tracks. That was the first and last time I would do that to Katie. I thought she would scream and then hit me playfully; I didn't realize she would scream and shiver in terror with tears streaming down her face. Men, do not prank your wives. You are not in a fraternity anymore, and she is not your roommate. Lesson learned.

Back to those college-group gatherings: The cabin in the woods scheme made for several nights of fun. However, because I was fresh out of college, it was hard to be perceived as the leader. I felt stuck in college, not like the middle school and college pastor I was hired to be. I think the church thought I would relate well to college students, but the truth was, I still was a college student. Single, living on my own, and going to work—it was the life of a bachelor, and I hated it.

High school and college gave me a sense of direction and time frame for my life. There was an end goal in sight each semester, always working toward a graduation of some sort. Once I graduated high school, I immediately started college. Then, after more semesters and summers, I eventually graduated from college, but I immediately started working full-time.

The rhythm of semester, break, semester, then summer ended abruptly. Life became this daunting forever task with ten days off a year. How was I supposed to go from twenty weeks off a year in college to ten days off? The transition was miserable.

I later found out that becoming a teacher was the way to address that dilemma (not to say teachers don't work their tails off during the school year). My personality type, described as a performer and a perfectionist, would find its fit in the teaching world. I have found that in these times of learning about one's calling and vocation, when it doesn't feel like the present is supposed to be permanent, feelings like doubt, fear, and anger can creep into the soul. In those periods of transition and growth, I project my anxieties on others, unable to show empathy or compassion. I isolate my heart out of fear of hitting a place of failure.

Hannah was unknowingly caught in the middle of two of the greatest transitional times of my life. One was a vocational dilemma, and the other was marriage and instant fatherhood. As difficult as she could be, I know she was also on the receiving end of my deepest insecurities.

This first night of hanging out in the cabin in the woods, I don't remember Kyle being there. There would be many more nights where I would get to spend time with him, but this first night was around the spa. A couple of guys and I were in our swimsuits in the hot tub. It was April in that forest town. Spring had started, but just barely. It was cold outside.

There were a couple of girls sitting around the spa sticking their legs in, and Katie was one of them. Technically, Katie wasn't in college, but she was college-age. Katie's friend, the one who babysat Kyle, knew Katie needed more friends during this time, so she invited Katie over to the house in the woods to make friends with the other girls in the group.

At the time, I felt no attraction to Katie because she had a kid, and she was still married. I did not know it then, but her marriage was in shambles. The reason Katie's friend invited her to hang out so much was to witness to her and show her how much life there was on the other side of what we perceive as a tragedy. Katie didn't fit the bill as one of our college students, but it worked out because we had a varying degree of ages and life stages in our group.

This friend, who knew Katie from high school, had the same friends from high school that Katie had, but Katie had lost touch with them. It was an easy sell for this friend to bring Katie along and introduce her to new friends and rekindle old relationships. She wanted Katie to know that God still loved her and had plans and dreams for her. Honestly, it had to be the Lord's work in this person's life to step outside of her comfort zone and not only hang out with Katie but be okay with basically co-parenting Kyle in his early years. Katie needed help, and her longtime friend was right beside her.

The only memory Katie has of this first night is me pointing out the shape of my chest hair to everyone. Selling my manly chest hair as the shape of a flower was of course not my goal at all, so I had named it the dragonfly. A line of hair with two wings sticking out on either side, it was a dragonfly from a bird's-eye view. If I were a superhero, I wouldn't need a costume, because my logo had already grown on my chest naturally. I would not only be saving lives but money as well—no need for a costume designer.

I always got a good laugh with that joke, and that was the same reaction I got from Katie. I should have known there was something more to her that night when all the other girls rolled their eyes in disgust and Katie just laughed. If a girl can laugh at the shape your hair makes on your chest, you know you've found yourself a keeper.

There were other nights where we would interact, but the interaction wasn't between Katie and me; it was between Kyle and me. It was as if this group of young college-aged people took in this family that just needed a little love. Kyle was easy to love. While the girls would hang out in a room, Kyle just wanted to run around and be one of the guys. He was turning two the summer I bonded with him, and I called him a man's man kind of kid. Kyle wanted to do whatever guy thing there was to do: baseball, football, basketball, soccer, hide and seek, trains, trampolines, and most of all, running. I was attracted to the amount of life and energy Kyle had. His laugh was unmistakable and contagious. As he started forming words and communicating, it was just so adorable.

The first time I was asked to babysit Kyle, it was so my youth-ministry-volunteer friend could take Katie to a Casting Crowns concert at the local fairground's amphitheater. Katie had been living with her parents, and they were both away. Kyle's father was not in the picture, and Kyle's other grandparents were busy. Katie was so disappointed she could not go, so my friend called me and cashed in a favor.

Our Saturday-night youth service involved games, worship, and a lesson. I was not part of any of those elements that particular evening. The idea of letting Kyle run around outside while the youth service was being self-run on the inside was great. Kyle and I played basketball for about half an hour. I thought he would want me to lift him up several times to make a shot. I did it once, but he didn't seem to care. So I made a shot and it haphazardly sunk into the net.

The immediate eruption of excitement from this big little child caught me off guard. He threw his fist in the air and just screamed: "Yeaaaa … again!" I made another shot, this one much more graceful, knowing I needed to make it in this time to elicit the same response. Much to my joy, his fist went up again, and "Yeaaaa" burst out of his lungs. Kyle just wanted to watch me make shots and cheer for me each time I made it.

Excitement for life is one of Kyle's greatest qualities. Skipping a few parts of the story, I eventually was able to adopt him and have him take my last name, the same as our three younger children. This was a dream Hannah had for me, but she would not live to see it. If Hannah were alive to witness my adoption of Kyle, she would be overjoyed. For me, it was a moment of regret turned to joy.

Hannah grew to love Kyle during our time in Colorado. Aunt Hannah, or Annanah as Kyle pronounced it, would be one of Kyle's best buds, and I know he remembers her in photographs. Annanah is how I taught Kyle about Heaven, Jesus, the Cross, and Redemption. Annanah's impact after her death still has ripple effects to this day.

Who is this kid? I thought to myself. I had never met a boy who would stand there and want me to make all the shots and then cheer for me with each basket. There was something different about Kyle, something that inspired me, that revealed to me the freedom of being a child—freedom from worries, burdens, and responsibilities that allow one to embrace the moment. Kyle fully lived in the present, with awe and wonder.

I wanted that freedom to live freely without worry. I was never that kind of kid; my mother called me a worrywart. There was a picture of me in a swing when I was two, and I had a worried look on my face. I do not know if you can have OCD at two, but clearly, I had a lot on my mind. *Why am I on this swing? Why are you taking a picture of me, and why in the world am I just in my underwear?* If I were to imagine Kyle in this same swing at two years of age, his mouth would be wide open with pure joy, his eyes glistening in the sun as he lost the feeling of gravity for a moment until his weight pulled him back down toward the ground.

Kyle was the opposite of me. He was the kid I dreamed of being— not a worry in the world, not a fear to hold onto. That kid was unstoppable. Well, unstoppable until you stopped the thing he was doing, and then the full range of emotion would come pouring out of him. Kyle's emotional highs were as deep as his lows.

We later began to understand how Kyle's world was affected by sensory processing disorder. His body craved input and stimulation of his senses more than his peers'. His disorder was what attracted me to him, and it also has, ironically, become my greatest challenge with him.

Kyle is now a preteen on the autism spectrum and the oldest of four, and he has great days and difficult days. His behavior is predictable; he must be given the same consequence a few dozen times before there is a change in behavior. Hannah would try to tell me what it was like to have ADHD when Kyle was given the diagnosis at the age of six. Her comments drove me crazy.

Hannah diagnosed herself with ADD only after Kyle's diagnosis. Overnight, she became the expert on what Kyle was going through and took it upon herself to inform me about my child. I wouldn't hear it; I hated letting Hannah think she was a know-it-all. Being in your twenties with ADD is not the same as having a child with ADHD. The hyperactive component is the challenge for the outside person looking in. Children with ADHD get into trouble because they are so impulsive that their behavior never goes unnoticed.

I couldn't pinpoint why Hannah's words bothered me so much until my mom mentioned she was trying to teach Hannah that you can't speak in a way that makes you the expert if you are not. My mom told her, "You must speak in a way that is an opinion that can be accepted or rejected." Hannah's hardest lessons came when people, including her siblings, rejected her opinion. She would take it as a rejection of her, which I now know is part of BPD.

I felt backed into a corner by Hannah; I had to accept her views on how to raise Kyle as a kid with special needs or I was rejecting her. It was a lose-lose scenario, and I did not have the patience for it. I didn't take the time to learn about BPD because I was trying to wrap my head around my own son's needs. I didn't realize that rejection was her biggest fear, and people with BPD place the people they love in scenarios where rejection is inevitable, only to be able to prove their point of rejection.

You could say people with BPD are their own worst enemies, creating situations that make it hard for the people closest to them not to reject, or at least distance, themselves. It's a self-fulfilling prophecy, and the person with BPD will always find a reason for blame. Ultimately, with Hannah, I was fighting the wrong battle. What I thought I needed was boundaries, but what I needed was to stop playing the game of rejection and blame. I would fight fire with fire, and that would drive the wedge between us even deeper.

After basketball with Kyle that first night of babysitting duty, as the service was ending and the students were leaving our youth building, Kyle was running around at full speed, which he had been doing for fifteen minutes. He made eye contact with me and started running toward me—to hug me, I presumed. Kyle was so close to me but did not see the protruding sidewalk edge that was popping up just a couple inches away. We have all had a million of these moments where we see the complete happiness in our children's eyes and, within a split second, the carefree world they are living in becomes flooded with tears.

Kyle could not stop crying for fifteen minutes, and rightly so. It's like the quote by Douglas Adams that my brother Alex would tell me jokingly: "It's not the fall that kills you, it's the sudden stop at the end." It was not the fall that hurt Kyle; it was the forehead to the sidewalk that left a blue goose egg the size of an actual goose egg on his forehead. My immediate thought was, *Well, I guess I'm not going to be able to babysit Kyle anymore.* I almost killed Katie's kid, and it had only been an hour and a half since she dropped him off.

I tried icing the injury, but there is no two-year-old on the planet who lets you place something cold on a newly formed bruise; I don't know why we as parents even try. Someone needs to invent a strap-on cold pack that we can put on children when they are asleep. I finally mustered up the courage to call my friend who was with Katie at the concert.

With panic and a good mix of concern and guilt, I tried to be as honest as possible when I got Katie on the phone. I didn't want to downplay the scenario that had unfolded minutes before. She laughed and assured me Kyle would be fine and was a tough kid. She was right; there would be several other incidents in his childhood years that would prove exactly how tough and flexible he was. The plan was for me to watch him until nine or ten that night, so I took him back to my one-bedroom condo and tried to entertain him by flipping my small coffee tables upside down and having him step from one to the other. He already was standing on top of them, and my genius idea was to have them placed upside down. I wasn't sure which would be worse: him falling off one or being impaled by one of the legs.

At about eight-thirty, I tried to put him to bed, in his onesie as instructed, but he kept coming out of my room. He wanted me to lie down with him, so I stretched out close beside him, and I just rubbed his head and sang to him. *Fatherhood must feel like this*, I thought. A small sense of purpose was confirmed in me that night. I hoped God would bring me a family someday. Lying next to Kyle was just perfect.

The song I sang is a song I often sing when no one else is around and when the child is young enough not to know it. It's an old *Psalty the Singing Songbook* song from the 1980s. It had always stuck with me since I was a child:

> Lord make me a servant,
> humble and meek.
> Lord let me lift up,
> those who are weak.
> And may the prayer of my heart always be,
> Make me a servant,
> Make me a servant,
> Make me a servant ... today!

I've sung this song to a few nieces and nephews and, of course, my children. Kyle was the first, and each baby since has been blessed with my unusual choice of a lullaby song they will never remember, from a movie they will never see. It has just been my secret.

I bonded with Kyle that night, having felt like he allowed me into his world of needing comfort to fall asleep. It was an honor to share, and to be honest, I do not know if he ever did fall asleep before Katie showed up. I do know that he did not make a sound the whole time.

When the ladies finally arrived, they were impressed that I had fed him, gotten him into his pajamas, and at least had him quietly in bed. They thanked me and said they had a blast. Then Katie carried Kyle out to the car. I think the darkness of night help hide the extra forehead that had grown on Kyle over the past several hours. I had dodged that bullet. I called it a successful first time babysitting the boy who eventually would have a greater impact on my life than I knew at the time. But it wasn't just my life that Kyle would change—it was Hannah's as well.

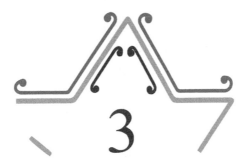

3

Broken Places

It was the Christmas Katie and I started our relationship. I had called my family a week before to tell them I was bringing over a special friend. A little boy would be accompanying her. Katie will not let it go to this day that I introduced her as "my friend Katie that I told you about" on Christmas Eve when I brought her and Kyle over to meet my family.

Well, honestly, a simple phone call to my family was not exactly the path I took. There was an underlying fear within me of my siblings' disapproval as well as that of my mother and stepdad. The only person I knew would not judge Katie was Hannah. I never feared her judgment of me because there was never any judgment given, which is something I overlooked about her. Maybe it was because I was her older sibling, or maybe it was something that came naturally to her. Either way, she had a deep sense of love and grace toward me, and Hannah would extend that to my "friend" and her son.

I first called my stepdad, asking for advice. I let him know there was a girl I liked, but—and it was a big but—she had a two-year-old son. He simply asked if she liked me in return and what the boy thought of me. I told him the story of how I met Kyle first. I'd had a vision of Kyle on a trip to Israel I had taken several months back, well before liking Katie.

I asked my stepdad if it was okay for me to pursue Katie, even though the final court date for her divorce was at the end of the month. I was not sure if what I was doing was the right thing—whether pursuing a married woman was morally wrong, even though she had physically and spiritually been separated for almost a year and had severed all ties except for a court date that was days away.

My stepdad was honest about the timing of his marrying my mom. It intertwined with my mom's divorce from my father when I was three. He said getting a divorce is a process; it is not clear-cut, and he recognized at the time that my mother needed help caring for her four children. Not that my father had it any easier when all four of us were with him, but my mom had sole custody, which meant we were living with her full time. My stepdad did not wait for the divorce to be finalized before pursuing a relationship with my mom.

Things had not worked out the way either of my biological parents had planned, and it seemed that separating was the most appropriate way to move forward in their lives. My mom received sole custody of my older three siblings and me, but my parents shared legal custody. There were monthly visitations, but all educational and medical decisions were made equally. Growing up, I did not understand that this division affected Hannah as my half-sister as much as it did my siblings and me. There are always negative ripples within a mixed family; no perfect scenario is played out. The need for grace within these types of homes is monumental—more than either parent, whether biological, step, adoptive, foster, or surrogate, can handle alone.

I felt I now had permission to pursue Katie, which was what I was seeking. One night early that December, before introducing her to my family, I tried to tell Katie I liked her. I did that lame thing that Christians do where we say, "Can I pray for you?" This was code for, "I'm too much of a wuss to tell you that I like you." However, after my conversation with my stepdad, I was free from my fear of judgment for pursuing a relationship with a technically married woman. I remembered that God did not care about pieces of paper; it was the spirit of the law, not the letter of the law, that mattered.

My stepdad said Katie needed to know how I felt. After my

floundering attempt at overspiritualizing my feelings for Katie, to which she said nothing, I tried again the following night. She has since reminded me on several occasions that I blew it that first night, and we laugh about it. "Is it okay that I pray for you," a direct quote by the way, became our inside joke—the first of many.

The following night was much better. I apologized for being vague the night before, and I told Katie I wanted to make my intentions clear. I liked her, and I wanted to date her. It sounds like I had a great sense of confidence in knowing how she would respond, but most of us are fearful of rejection. The only reason I knew she liked me back was that Katie's and my mutual friend had answered a key question a few days before.

As any smart young man knows (or any middle-school boy, for that matter), if you want to know if a girl likes you, ask her friends. However, I was not a middle-school boy; I was a cunning and crafty man in my twenties. The question I carefully constructed for my friend was, "Is Katie ready to date again?" This neither forced Katie's friend to betray any feelings Katie may have shared with her and provided her with a nonhurtful way of letting me down.

The other reason I did not ask "Does Katie like me?" is because of the personality type of my friend. She said things exactly as they came to her mind, so I wanted to make sure I could receive an answer that would hurt less if it was one of rejection. I would rather hear "She is not ready to date" than "No, she doesn't like you." My friend would have answered it either way, so I made sure to set myself up for a soft blow.

There is a tactical benefit in dealing with a blunt person. Blunt people should rarely be offended. Don't be shocked if people reject an unwanted opinion. Until achieving a desirable response, a blunt person will continue to offer up a different opinion. Hannah was like that somewhat; she would offer up her unsolicited opinion but would not follow the rest of the rule that the blunt person's opinion may be soundly rejected. Instead, Hannah would take it as a personal attack on her character. In Hannah's mind, people did not like or accept her if her opinion was not accepted or followed.

I never understood this and tried to explain it to Hannah the week before we moved away from Colorado Springs, away from the house on Stone Fence Drive. I hurt Hannah that day; I hurt her in a way that, for many years, I would be unable to forgive myself for. My words were justified, in that I was correct in my accusations and name-calling, but as my mom said to me, "Just because you are right, doesn't mean you are right." Understanding that paradox is essential in a truly loving and forgiving relationship, and I understand that now too late.

Perhaps that is a reason for some of my regret. There is a time to be blunt, and there is a desire to be reactionary to a blunt person, but that doesn't not mean it is the right course of action. I wish I could have framed my questions to Hannah better and responded in a way that was the opposite of how I perceived her at the time.

Katie's response to my more clearly laid-out advances that second night was a large beaming smile. Her eyes were captivating and revealed everything she wanted me to feel and know. I literally could see love in them; I could also see hurt, pain, regret, fear, anger, laughter, joy, sarcasm, and everything in between. Her feelings for me were unmistakable in the way she looked at me.

What was different about Katie from the previous girls I had dated? She never once revealed to me her feelings, nor did she behave in a way that implied she liked me as more than a friend. She was the quiet killer; she wooed me with her laugh, charm, and friendship. A year before my infatuation with Katie, I had dated a friend from college. The problem with that relationship was that I had not asked for it. At the time, I was trying to start a relationship with a different girl. However, when my college friend told me she liked me, I had to see if there was something there. Long story short, one of my sisters informed me that

I was moving from relationship to relationship too fast and that I was moving too fast with Katie. This hurt, and I ended up snapping back at her, which began a broken relationship with my older sister that went unresolved for several years. Everything I learned in my relationship with Hannah would eventually save my relationship with my other sister, but it took years.

That night, I told my older sister I did not want her to speak into my life. I was an adult now, and she didn't have the right to tell me who to date. In my sister's defense, she did not know how serious I was about Katie and that my intentions were to more than just date but to marry her. I don't think I told anyone that Katie and I were deciding whether or not we wanted to get married as early as possible for Kyle's sake.

I took offense at my older sister's reproach and approach because she was one of two people in the family who always seemed to have it all together. In my mind, the twins were the anomaly of my mixed family. They were such a powerhouse: a duo who from the outside made the rest of us look like mere mortals. I do not think Hannah or I were the black sheep; I think the twins were just extraordinary golden sheep while the other three of us were the normal ones.

My older brother had a different role. He was not a sheep at all. He was the family guinea pig, as are many oldest children. It's their blessing and their curse. Neither Hannah nor I felt like we measured up to any of our older siblings. We had that in common—or at least, I thought we did before Colorado. I would come to realize that Hannah's opinion of me had shifted into the same category she and I had perceived the oldest three siblings to inhabit. This is another regret on my part, being so insecure that I did not see my apparent greatness, but Hannah did, because she had put me in the golden sheep category.

Never in a million years would I equate my standing in the family with the status of the twins. I struggled with being overweight. I was hearing-impaired. I had a speech impediment until I was seven. I was never a straight-A student. I was not great at sports, although I did finally stick it out in Taekwondo and earn my black belt at seventeen.

My view of myself was that I was just normal, but Hannah's view of me was that I was extraordinary.

The fact that I had to overcome so much is how she measured my success. In her mind, not giving up on life and pushing back made me great, and that earned me the title of the golden sheep. It hurts when someone you hold in high esteem speaks down to you, which is what I did with Hannah in Colorado. I was the golden sheep who was blind to his uniqueness, the one Hannah admired but who began to stonewall her at a rapidly increasing rate during the last five years of her life.

A few years earlier, I had brought home another girl to meet the family. This girl, I now believe, was unintentionally misleading me. I think she was lonely and just enjoyed my company, while I was looking for "the one." Feelings of love can make a person foolish. Forced love and the false sense of love are just two sides of the same coin.

Hannah saw it; she told me later she did not think this girl was right for me. She knew my intentions in bringing this girl home to meet my sister, my mom, and my stepdad, and Hannah could sense that this girl did not feel the same way. Hannah could read me (which I did not like), and she had a good sense of what people were safe for me. I do not know why this bothered me; perhaps it was a case of the older sibling not believing the younger sibling had grown up and had legitimate thoughts, feelings, and knowledge of the world around her. My older siblings sometimes treated me this way, and it was how I eventually treated Hannah.

What does she know? I would think to myself. However, she did sniff out the bad girls in my life, and when she met Katie, her sixth sense would prove handy. It seemed that no girls were good enough for me, because Hannah was protective of me. Hannah's protection of me was something I did not learn about until I met with her therapist after Hannah passed away, which is another regret I carry. Hannah's radar was spot-on. Katie was a safe person.

There was a lot to talk about that night, because in my mind, I was concerned not only for Katie's heart but also for the sweet boy who called me Joey and was sleeping in the next room. I did not want to propose on the same night that I was asking her out for a simple date. I was trying to find a very careful balance. I wanted Katie to know that I intended to date her in order to marry her because I wanted Kyle to know that I was committed to sticking around. The longer we took to date in the traditional sense, the older Kyle would get, and I did not want him confused by my presence in their lives.

Katie accepted my terms of pursuing marriage by allowing me to be the one to bring up the topic again and ask when it was time. I was not trying to be chauvinistic or controlling; I did not want Katie to feel like she had to do anything other than be herself. Katie's job was to respond to my advances and let me know if I was going too fast or too slow.

A mere four months later, I would propose, and six months after that we would get married. I think we did well with sticking to the plan. I pursued Katie, and she let me. I admitted I loved her first, and she let me. I told her I wanted to decide on the timing of marriage, and she did not stop me. Every step of the way, Katie was directing my steps by allowing me to chart the course we were taking.

Some people see this as outdated; they think that the woman should be able to lead and be equal in all aspects of a relationship. However, I was not looking for that kind of relationship. I did not want to date someone who had the same personality as me. I wanted someone who was willing to both let me lead and lead me through her response to me. What clicked was Katie's confidence in what she did not have to say.

Even when it came time for me to start disciplining Kyle, Katie was ready and trusted me. Kyle was young enough that I could still be a natural father/authority figure in his life. I just needed to start helping Katie enforce her rules. Disciplining Kyle came more naturally than I had thought it would, and my love for Kyle would shape my desire for him to respect and honor his mother.

Kyle captivated Hannah too. If I loved kids, she loved kids ten times more. Not only did I get Hannah's approval of Katie, but Hannah fell in love with Kyle as I had—the oldest niece or nephew for her to put all her talent with children to the test. Looking back, I can see the amazing blessing and impact she had on Kyle, and I can also see my folly and jealousy.

I wanted to be Kyle's parent and arrogantly rejected many of Hannah's ideas about him. I made my relationship with Hannah all or nothing. It set it up to where the only way Hannah could please me was to behave the way I wanted her to. I became the controlling one, and the disguise I used was being a new husband and father.

My boundaries with Hannah were shackles to prevent her from truly being a part of my new family. I would not allow Hannah to tell me how to do my job. My wife, on the other hand, would become Hannah's best friend for a few different seasons of life, and Kyle would be Hannah's focus as an aunt. It helped when it came time for Katie and me to work, but for some reason, I did not want Hannah's opinion on or advice regarding my family. My stepdad eventually told me that it was part of being in my twenties, responding to problems in arrogance, which manifests in anger or over-aggression.

The desire to protect Katie and Kyle from the turmoil they had experienced as well as the need to prove myself as a husband and a father would change and then break the bond Hannah and I once had, because I was a ticking time bomb. When we decided to leave Colorado, I took a great swing at the problems that had festered during our ten-month stay on Stone Fence Drive. There was an avoidable confrontation; however, in my arrogance and cruelty of knowing I was leaving Hannah, I took a stab at fixing my frustrations with her. I confronted her, without compassion, about everything that bothered me about her, with no consideration as to how my words affected her.

My mother told me the next day that during my bombardment of accusations, she sat there in silence and disbelief as I hurled my best arguments as to why Hannah needed to stay out of my business. My mother was shocked that the young man she raised was the one taking such brutal, offensive maneuvers against her youngest daughter. My mom told me she regretted not standing up for Hannah and that I was the bully, calling my sister names with a complete lack of consideration or empathy. I tried to do a half-apology for my tone but not for my intent or words, but my mother saw right through me, and her words still linger in my head: "I didn't know what to say at the moment. I was in shock at how you spoke to your sister."

After my small attempt at defending my actions, my mother would make a statement that I still wrestle with today: "If you have to justify your words or actions, then you are doing something wrong."

I constantly think about this statement as one of those lessons learned as an adult, but it immediately put me on the defensive. For years, I was defensive about the need to justify my actions, thinking of scenarios at work, with my friends or family, where my justification did not make my actions wrong. I had missed my mother's point that day with Hannah; she prodded my pride. My arrogance in proving to Hannah why she was wrong, and the way I approached her as a person—telling and not teaching—was my error.

My mother, in her wisdom, was teaching me still the lesson she had been teaching me my entire life, but this time she had worded the message as an adult should hear it: two wrongs do not make a right. If I must justify my wrong behavior, then I have erred and made the timeless mistake of believing my anger justified my words. Did my sister try to put herself in the middle of an issue that did not concern her? Yes. However, my confrontation that day was more profoundly wrong than I could have imagined.

The Colorado Confrontation was a wedge that would divide me and Hannah for years. I regret my choice to shut out Hannah, but at the same time, I am not sure how I could have responded differently. Could I have changed the outcome of Hannah's life had I behaved differently? Would Hannah be alive today if I had changed the way I treated her during those months in Colorado and the years that followed? I think everyone who experiences unexpected loss asks that question, especially parents of children lost to tragedy.

This depth of regret can become unbearable for some. You are supposed to outlive your children. The burden can be so great that taking one's life seems to be the only escape from the pain. I have both pastored and taught several teenagers who have lost a sibling or a parent for various reasons. The most heartbreaking have been the ones who lost an older sibling to suicide and, years later, would lose a parent to suicide because the parent could never overcome the guilt and shame of having lost a child.

Individuals who take their lives are unable to see the moment or the future, only the past and the regret and guilt. When I think of the worst circumstances in life, these students come to mind, and what is amazing is to see that it is possible to choose joy in the midst of this kind of tragedy. I never expect a teenager to respond well in this kind of circumstance, and I have been surprised by those who do. These students understand; they see the place where death and life connect. They experience something only they can understand, and in the midst of it, they accept the death and embrace the life God has given them.

One particular student comes to mind, and others would never know his story unless you asked him. He said, "It was God that brought my mother and me through the darkest of our pain." This young man found his joy when he realized God had an individual purpose for his life.

I have come to realize I cannot play the what-if game. Finding purpose after a tragedy is difficult, but this deep work of the soul can drive you further than anyone else that has not experienced this kind of pain. A shattered heart restored can be ten times stronger with ten times the amount of endurance to handle any circumstance. The key is to find out how to have your heart experience the art of *kintsukuroi*, which translated from Japanese means "golden repair." This ancient practice of repairing pottery using a glue substance mixed with varying valuable minerals like gold represents something broken but restored into something greater.

Every culture recognizes brokenness. In his book *A Farewell to Arms*, in response to the devastation of the events of the Great War, Ernest Hemingway eloquently describes what happens to even the most courageous and brave: "The world breaks everyone and afterward many are strong at the broken places." Either you become better from tragedy or you die from it. If we ignore our fallenness, then we are blind to the possibility of renewal, and possibly greater. If you do not admit you need rescuing from anything, you wrongly believe you do not need a rescuer.

If we fail to recognize our shortcomings, we fail to realize that we can and must do better and be better people. Who is it that can repair a shattered heart and make it even more beautiful than it was before so that we can see strength within "the broken places"? Is it something you do yourself, or is it something you trust the cosmic forces of chance and luck to do? The recognition of our brokenness starts the process of healing, but there is still further to go.

It would make sense to go back to the Potter, the one who made our heart to begin with, and ask Him to repair it. As the Psalmist proclaims, "He heals the brokenhearted and binds up their wounds ..." (Psalm 147:3). When God heals it, He makes it better than it was before. The Bible talks about a greater transformation, more than the healing of our heart. The prophet Ezekiel says, "I will give you a new heart and put a new spirit in you; I will remove from you your heart of stone and give you a heart of flesh" (Ezekiel 36:36). The prophecy is about what has already occurred and is continuing to occur in the lives of those who have fixed their eyes upon their Creator, who recognizes, validates, and spends careful time repairing our broken hearts and mending together the shattered pieces of our lives. Then He transforms what remains into a new heart along with a new spirit which the coming of the Holy Spirit fulfills.

There is something extremely profound about the Gospel message for the hurting. It does not present simply a self-help journey to healing. The Gospel message invites a deep connection to the Spirit, which connects us all. We must not water down the Christian faith to represent a ticket to heaven. That would put to shame Jesus's life, death, resurrection, and His eventual return. He is coming back for those who are whole and those in the process of healing by the power of the same Spirit that brought Him back to life.

We who profess Jesus as Lord have God in us, continually strengthening us in the places that are weak and completely renewing us through His Spirit. There is so much work to do between the here-and-now and the eternity to come. We cannot lose hope for what tomorrow brings.

My actions may or may not have contributed to my sister's death, but I carry the belief with me that they did. I think God allowed me to experience this to understand my stepdad just a little bit. I think most of the heartache that I have now is not about my loss of Hannah but about seeing the brokenness in my stepdad. I know he constantly lives in a state of regret, mourning, sorrow, and blame. His only blood child is gone. How can he not feel the angst of failure?

I have days where I empathize with him to the point of tears, and I am crying out to God for him, praying that God would strengthen him when his grief seems unbearable. My stepdad carries himself well; I do not fear that he will take his life, but I grieve that he will never be the same. I cannot expect him to be. Everything in our lives has changed, and this is our new reality—this is *his* new reality.

I have heard it said that the last part of becoming an adult is to see and accept the imperfection of your parents. As children, we see them as impenetrable and indestructible, but when a divorce happens or some experience abuse, we realize early on how imperfect they are. Most see the imperfection of their parents when they, too, become adults and realize that their parents do not have life figured out either. Taking ownership of your own life and taking the giant step into adulthood that involves recognizing that your parents were guessing too is difficult.

It has been even more difficult to see my parents grieve over the loss of their child, my sister. It does not bother me that they are not perfect and broken; what does bother me is the knowledge that I cannot fix them. They do not expect me to, but when people we love are hurting, our natural desire is to try.

It takes a lot of discernment to recognize your place in the life of a person who is grieving. I have learned more about marriage by watching my parents carry each other's burdens than through anything else. I cannot predict the future after writing all this; maybe their marriage will fall apart. They learned through counseling that statistically, there is an 80 percent chance that their marriage will end in divorce, after losing a child. But I have great hope that they will continue to grieve together rather than apart.

As we live together in our marriages and families, so with death we should grieve together. Grieving is the burden that families who have lost loved ones carry. The process of grief, and the fact that we grieve differently, is a challenge. I will be honest: I do not think I understand my siblings' grief, nor have I shared mine with them. We do not always see each other, and I think we do not want to always have to talk about death when we are together. We have so many children between the four of us, and we see so much life in front of us. I hope I can open that door by sharing my story with them someday, and I pray that they find themselves and their perspectives in my story.

My wife understands my grief, and she grieves as well, having become close to Hannah during our years of marriage. I am grateful for that, and it's possible that this understanding has made a difference in how we have responded to each other's needs through this loss. Several years after Hannah died, my brother's wife lost her brother and nephew in a car accident. My brother, in his brokenness, was able to understand and, in some sense, relate to his wife on an empathetic level. Experiencing death without the accompanying understanding of your spouse is hard on both people. One is stuck in grief while the other does not see the need to stop and grieve or is more easily ready for life to move on.

I think this is the heart of all grief when you lose a child, sibling, parent or spouse: initially wishing that time would stop so we never have to move on. The proximity of the pain of loss is so close that the person who has lost someone wants the hurt to stop but also does not wish to have the passage of time distance them from the last moments they had with their loved one. The more time that passes, the more fear of forgetting our loved ones grows: what they looked like, how they talked, what it felt like to embrace them. As time passes, the way we recollect events changes, and we do not have the person we lost to help us sort out those memories.

Time heals all wounds, some people say. Unfortunately, with grief, time is the enemy. Each holiday, each anniversary of the day of passing, the day of the funeral, even the days leading up to and after the death are constant moments in time that bring hated but necessary pain to the heart. We want the pain to stop, but when the pain stops, we feel that we are numb. If we, in our hearts, feel disconnected from the person we lost, we allow ourselves to feel the pain on purpose.

Time does not heal the wound of death, and the change with time can make this new reality unbearable. We wish we had had more time with our loved one; we wish time could have stood still for just a moment before death, and we wish the time without them would be less. We cry at the grave of our loved one, "Why have you left me? The time without you is impossible to face alone." Time is no friend to those who have lost or to those who know they will be losing someone as the aroma of near death lingers in the air.

I sometimes wonder if I would like to have known Hannah was

going to die. Would it have been easier to prepare myself had she had cancer or some other terminal illness? Is it better to rip open a wound slowly as if done surgically without anesthesia or to experience the stab as unsuspected, forceful, and gut-wrenching? I would prefer no wound at all, and I do not know if one scenario is less painful than the other.

I think the degree of death's damage has to do with four levels of relationship to the deceased:

1. The first level is your proximity to the deceased. Is it someone in the news, a friend of a friend, a grandparent, or someone in your household?
2. The second is the loved one's phase of life before passing away. Each age range carries a very different burden.
3. The third level involves the story the loved ones were living at the time of passing. Were they depressed; were they on track to a successful career; did they have a family; were they young and innocent?
4. The fourth level is how they died, which can shift the balance of difficulty when determining the impact of another's death on oneself.

I know losing a grandparent is hard because you are also losing a longstanding leader of the family, a parent, a sibling, but there is such great comfort in knowing the life they lived was a long one. Grieve, be sad, mourn the loss of these loved ones, but know that your goal is to become like them someday.

I cannot imagine the burden of reponsibility that the suicide of a teenager must bring for a parent. Could the death have been prevented? This line of thinking can lead a parent to impossible places. Reconciling a random, horrible, and out-of-control chaotic chance of fate in one's mind can create storms of varying degrees. It could be cancer or another type of devastating illness, all of which we have no control over. We will shake our fists at God, and we will try to shift the blame to Him. However, there is no scapegoat for parents in these circumstances. It can break them, and the question is where the pieces will fall. It's not impossible to come back from this, but if there is no landing pad to catch the falling pieces, the damage can be irreparable from a human perspective.

The ground beneath us, our foundation, our convictions and beliefs about life and its value, will determine the impact of the falling pieces of our lives. The pain of death's sting directly correlates to our proximity to the one who died, the phase of life and story of the one who died, and the manner in which our loved one died. These four things will determine not only the depth of the wound and its duration but the size of the scar that remains.

4

Making A Move

After I had introduced my immediate family to my "friend" at Christmas, Katie and I waited a couple more weeks until we made our relationship official. It was not until New Year's Eve that Katie's divorce finalized. Katie's ex-husband did not show up to any part of the process of Katie leaving or divorcing him. All Katie wanted was Kyle, so she asked for full legal custody, and her ex-husband agreed, since he had already moved on to a new relationship. It was clear to her that she'd made the right move.

Even though I had my mom's, stepdad's, and sibling's approval, I worried about my position at my church as a youth pastor, so I thought it would be safer if we didn't take our relationship further until after her divorce. I think she understood my position, since I was open with my reasoning. It is a hard line to walk when you are in a ministry position, because Christians in ministry are held to a higher moral standard publicly and by God—than a Christian who is not in ministry.

When reading the Gospels, we get the picture that everyone must follow the same moral standard. However, when it comes to church leadership, there is no room for error with these standards. Not that the shift is unbiblical: Paul tells both Titus and Timothy in the New Testament that the people they are to find as elders should meet certain qualifications. Paul makes the distinction between believers, and that distinction is maturity. It is possible to be a Christian stuck in sin as an immature believer. However, Christians who have authority must be mature believers.

In our culture, perception is reality, and I didn't want someone to falsely assume that I was dating a woman who was in an active marriage relationship. Was I ashamed that I liked a girl who had a son? Never. I was afraid someone would misconstrue our relationship with this false perception. I felt it would save us a lot of unnecessary grief if Katie and I just stayed friends who talked a lot until her divorce was final on December 31. What changed the morning of December 31 was fully manifested that New Year's Eve.

Katie came to my office after her court appointment with a gleam in her eye. She showed me the paperwork as I asked her how everything went. She said it was easy; the judge awarded her custody and even granted her child support with arrears going back to the time of filing paperwork, which was the previous summer. As well, her ex-husband was responsible for Kyle's health care, dental care, and any outstanding bills since their separation. For a single mom who had been balancing work and a two-year-old with the help of her parents, this was a huge blessing.

Nevertheless, in the grand scheme of things, the monthly child support didn't even begin to cover expenses for Kyle. I would forgo years of medicine and therapy for myself so that we could afford Kyle's medicine. We realized that what was best for Kyle was not to force his biological father into an unwanted father-son relationship. If we went after the man for money owed outside of the child support that was already being garnished from his wages by the state, it would rock the boat, and we didn't know what the consequences would be. If he didn't want to see Kyle, then we were not about to breach this sacred silence on his end for money.

Our decision would pay off years later when he would allow me to adopt Kyle uncontested. To stand in front of a judge with two new children in hand and hear a judge declare that Kyle would be my legal child was the long game Katie and I were playing. It represented years of praying, hoping, living within our means, and letting go bitterness and contempt. My biggest fear was losing Katie and then, by default, losing Kyle. By the time we had two more siblings for Kyle, the thought of losing custody of Kyle was heartbreaking.

My stepdad would often echo this sentiment about us four children. If my mom died, he would lose the four of us older children, and Hannah would lose us too. It was something I had never considered about my childhood—how the dynamic of visitation between my siblings with our father impacted Hannah, our half-sister. There were many similarities between Hannah and Kyle, and I think Hannah understood the worst of it. God spared Kyle from it, and Hannah knew Kyle had been spared.

Back in my office after the conversation about the logistics of what had transpired in court that day, Katie looked at me with a smile and said, "Does this mean I can be your girlfriend now?" The slight hint of a giggle that can only come from a smitten girl warmed my heart.

I finally had found someone who wanted me as much as I wanted her. Maybe that's what I was waiting for: her response after her divorce. I wanted her to be a free woman who freely wanted to be with me, not because she needed me but because she wanted me. With no strings attached, she was ready for me now, and I was ready for her.

It was the evening of New Year's Eve, and we were with the rest of our small town watching a lit-up giant pine cone drop from the second story of a historic hotel and bar. I was ready to act. Of course, I would kiss her; there was no better time to profess my feelings for her. I wanted to make it crystal clear I was all in, and I wasn't slowing down. I had a very clear mission and goal: I was going to marry Katie someday, and I was going to be Kyle's dad. The only thing holding us back was time.

The next months would unfold very quickly from a proposal to a wedding to the big decision to leave my hometown and pursue a degree at Denver Seminary in Colorado. We were not *falling* in love; we were *growing* in love. *Falling* seems to be an unrealistic, no-strings-attached, cloud nine experience. With Kyle in the equation from the beginning, we had expectations grounded in reality. We were growing in love with realistic expectations about marriage because we were parents.

The timing of my acceptance into seminary was not an accident. I had applied the year before meeting Katie, but my application did not get processed. The reason was probably God, yet at the time, I felt it was my fault. I didn't hear from them for almost six months. In that time, I gave up my plans of going to Colorado and assumed something else would turn up. The crazy thing about timing is that if I had enrolled for that semester, I would have left before I had the chance to find love in my relationship with Katie and Kyle. I had been ready to pack my bags and get out of my hometown. The ministry at my church was changing, and I was changing too. I'd never had a formal Bible education, so it felt like the time was right. When I didn't hear back from the seminary, I just forgot about it.

When Katie and I started dating, and I became involved more and more in Kyle's life, we found a new reason to leave town, and seminary came back on the table of options. It was first just a general discussion of where we saw ourselves in the immediate future, where we wanted to be in ten years, and what our lives would look like once our kids were out of the house. Yes, we discussed kids. We both wanted Kyle to have siblings, and we both had a similar number in mind: three or four.

Once you start having these deep discussions, the other set of logical questions are all the practical ones: Are we ready individually? Are we at a place in our maturity to be an independent family? Can we provide for ourselves? Should one of us work or both of us? What are our long-term expectations of each other and do they align? How do we view our marriage fifty years down the road?

We had most of our questions already answered when it came time to go through the premarital counseling that our church provided the summer before our wedding. One big thing I remember from our premarital class was the lesson that if we wouldn't fly a plane without proper training, we shouldn't try to navigate the course of marriage without the same preparation and ongoing maintenance required to make the trip. It was just over ten months of preparation from making my first move by first kissing Katie that New Year's Eve until we finally kissed at the altar. It was a crash course for sure, but I think we did more training and planning than most couples do who have engagements that last a year or longer. A lot of couples spend their time planning the perfect wedding day, but we were planning our life together, especially because of Kyle. We were making decisions knowing we needed a solid plan for Kyle, and the firmer we were, the better off we would be.

I called Denver Seminary back and asked about my application. They apologized for my application getting misplaced, and I finally got an interview, which was encouraging. The committee accepted my application because they sensed my calling and wanted to be a part of growing me along the way.

My parents and Hannah lived in Colorado Springs, a forty-five-minute drive from the school, and we could live in their entire four-room basement. It was where Hannah was living, but when she heard we wanted to move in, she didn't hesitate to move upstairs to the guest bedroom. I never thanked her for moving out of her space, one that had been hers for five years.

I had this impression of her as she lived in Colorado with my parents that she had a sense of entitlement with them. Somehow, she could "mooch" off them forever—eating their food, spending their money, always doing things first and asking questions later. In our own move to Colorado, I didn't even see how my behavior and expectations toward my parents were the same as Hannah's. I began to feel entitled to live in the basement and invade Hannah's place. I was older than Hannah, and I was in a different stage of life than she was. I had a family now, so in my head I deserved the bigger space in the house. I was thankful to my parents, but none of that gratitude was extended toward Hannah.

I expected Hannah to grow up and become an adult, but I still held us to the rules we acted upon as children: everything needed to be fair. I was very ungrateful for the things Hannah would do once we moved there, because I would only see it as a gift from my parents, not her. I regret not having the humility to express gratitude toward her. In actuality, it was Hannah's life and space that we invaded.

I proposed to Katie on top of a mountain that overlooked our city, along a hiking trail. Before long, we had a date, a chapel, and a reception. Things were falling into place just fine. For us, it was confirmation that God was leading us down the path he wanted us to follow. Advice someone gave us during this time was: "What you bring into the marriage regarding your relationship will be what you have when the kids leave the house someday."

We knew that we were best friends. Whether doing something together or nothing together, we just enjoyed being the one that the other could confide in. When the time comes and it is just Katie and me for the first time, we will get back the "years that the locusts have eaten," as my mom often says of life after a difficult circumstance (Joel 2:25b).

The time many couples have before children is time without the responsibility that comes with having kids. That is time Katie and I never had but look forward to enjoying someday. Even though my instant fatherhood was a major part of our marriage, Katie and I made sure that what we were bringing into it was something worth having fifty years down the road.

With that in mind and advice given, we took the plunge into marriage less than a year after we started dating. It is always better to chart a course and go, allowing God to guide you, than to stay still. He cannot take you anywhere if you aren't moving.

I didn't notice the absence of my sister during my wedding reception. Hannah had gotten a migraine, and so my stepdad had taken her back to the hotel. They both missed the entire reception. When I found out later, I was frustrated; this wasn't the first time Hannah happened to have a migraine during a family event. There was a need in Hannah's subconscious for my stepdad's attention and a fear of being lost in the crowd. Hannah was highly sensitive to any lack of attention or moments that were not about her in any fashion.

Getting attention from her mom and dad, I felt, was a way for Hannah to feel valued or not forgotten. I kept track; I couldn't let it go. At every wedding, every graduation, every baby shower, like clockwork, Hannah would feel unwell. I held that against her for years, and I ended up confronting her with it during the Colorado confrontation.

"You can't always play the victim, Hannah," I said.

The words pierced right through her eyes and tears came flowing down. My mom was silent, in complete disbelief at the name-calling from her son to her daughter. Those were just a few of the hurtful words and actions that came pouring out of me after years of bottled up frustration toward Hannah.

The Colorado confrontation was, and still is, my greatest regret when it comes to Hannah. In my defensiveness and my role as a self-perceived adult and self-declared truth teller, I would cut my sister's already fragile self-esteem to shreds. Why? Pride, arrogance, ignorance, delusion, lack of empathy, or all of the above. I felt that she was somehow robbing me of time that my mom and stepdad should have been able to focus on their other children. Hannah had lived with them her entire life, so why in these celebratory events did she need their exclusive attention? I held her to the same expectation that I held myself and everyone else to. I expected Hannah to act and behave normally.

That was part of the problem with my perception of her. The way Hannah experienced the world around her was very abnormal, and I failed to see that. My mother had mentioned several times Hannah's diagnosis of Borderline Personality Disorder before they moved to Colorado, but I didn't pay attention or seek to understand it. I wasn't sure what it was, and from my perspective, it was just a disorder she needed to work through. I gave no thought to how it affected me or the larger problem of how my actions, words, and behavior toward Hannah could feed into her disorder.

If I could go back and know what I know now, I would like to think I would at least have had empathy if nothing else—maybe allow myself to understand her inner turmoil. All I saw in Hannah was someone who was my equal in bad life circumstances that she often caused herself. I believed we should be held to the same standards and expectations of life. I was born with a hearing impairment; life wasn't easy for me, so why should I have to cater to her problems?

It wasn't love that I felt. That would be made clear in the years to come. I had my deep insecurities and imperfections to work out, and the reality of Hannah's death is that it became the clearest mirror to my soul, providing the deepest of reflections on myself and our relationship.

I don't think I would understand her even now if she were alive. It was only in Hannah's death, and after her death, that her story would unravel, and the truth of her pain would soften and break my hardened heart. To love someone, even if you think you are right and the other person is wrong, means sometimes you must allow that person to hurt you. To let down your guard and all your defenses for someone you love is the hardest thing to do. "Wounds from a friend can be trusted ..." as the old Proverb goes (Proverbs 27:6a). It would turn out that my relationship with Hannah foreshadowed other relationships in my life to come.

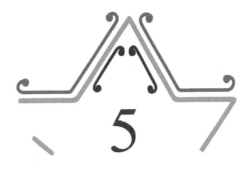

5

Traversing New Territory

I woke up at two in the morning and thought to myself, "We might as well start driving, and then Katie can drive after she sleeps."

It was just over a month since our wedding, and we were making our move to the house on Stone Fence Drive in Colorado where my parents and sister had lived for five years. We lived in their remodeled basement while I attended seminary in a suburb of Denver called Littleton. I would only have to drive there two or, at most, three times a week. Two of my classes would be online, so that helped cut down the amount of time I had to be on campus.

I'd enrolled for the spring semester because we wanted as much time as possible to settle into our new life before the work began. We saved all our wedding gifts and money to take with us to Colorado to furnish our little basement. By *little*, I mean it felt little because of its low ceiling. It consisted of two bedrooms, a makeshift kitchen area, and a living room, and it worked perfectly for a two-year plan while I went to school. Free rent and financial aid allowed us to eat, pay for school, and have money for our day-to-day needs.

I also still owned the one-bedroom condo in our hometown from before we got married. I was hoping I could make money on the rent, but I needed to hire a property-management company to take care of the tenants, and we ended up breaking even each month. We had what we needed, though. We were in debt to school loans, but we were content.

Once we settled in, I must be honest, Kyle didn't always stay in our basement with us. Truth be told, he ran all around the house, and my mom, stepdad, and especially Hannah just loved on him and cared for him beyond what I could have asked. One of the things Hannah would later tell me was that she wished I would validate all the time she invested in Kyle, but at the time, I felt inexplicably entitled to it. Of *course* she had to help with Kyle; she was living at home, dependent on my mom and stepdad just like I was, so what was the difference between us? Why should I show her gratitude for something that comes with the territory of living at home?

Therein lay the change in our relationship: in five years of living apart, I grew up, while Hannah's life remained the same. Our expectations were different; mine had changed, and hers had not. Hannah expected our lives to fit together just like they did before she, my mom, and my stepdad moved away from our small town to Colorado, and I was left alone. I had my abandonment issues after they left, and I hardened my heart toward life in general to numb my pain. I never realized how important family was until they left me during my senior year of college. In my mind, I was supposed to leave them on my terms, not the opposite.

During that five years, I stopped being the brother Hannah once knew. In his place, she found an apathetic shell of a man who withheld his emotions from her, sometimes on purpose. I thought our time on Stone Fence Drive would be a return to life as usual, but for Hannah, it was bittersweet. Katie would be an amazing sister-in-law to Hannah, and Kyle would love his Annanah (Aunt Hannah) so sweetly. But bitterness was my contribution to her life. If there was ever a person who scrutinized and picked apart another person's actions, it was me, and it started almost as soon as we got there.

The four of us were at the mall walking around thinking of Christmas presents and looking for home furnishings. Katie and I had invited Hannah along for shopping and possibly lunch. Hannah declared during the car ride that she wanted Taco Bell. I said that sounded fine, but we wanted to do our shopping first. After walking around for a while, we came to the food court, and I suggested maybe we could eat lunch at the mall and get it over with and go home.

Hannah said again that she wanted Taco Bell, and Katie didn't care either way. Kyle was getting ready to crash, and I was tired of walking, and it didn't seem like we were going to agree on anything definitive. Everything in Colorado Springs is so spread out; what should be a ten-minute drive judging by the location on a map took twice the time because of the direction and sheer size of some of the main roads. I decided I was tired and just wanted to go home. We had to walk all the way back to the car, and I wasn't about to get lost trying to find a Taco Bell for Hannah. In my head, I decided for the four of us even though only one of us—Hannah—cared about the outcome. The rest of us were ready to be home and call it a day.

In my mind, everything was fine; it was just another day in a new place. However, this was not the case for Hannah. She confronted me later that day about not going to Taco Bell. I was shocked; out of all the things I could do wrong in life, my sister was upset that I didn't take her to Taco Bell when I said I would. I thought back to the events that had transpired at the mall and before then, and I didn't understand Hannah's feelings. They were irrational. It was one meal out of thousands, and what was most important to me was getting my three-year-old home for his nap. I couldn't possibly drop everything to make sure my twenty-year-old sister, who can drive herself, had her expectations met for the day.

I quickly shut her down, half apologized, and said I had made a decision that was best for *my family*. There it was: the words came out, and I didn't realize the impact they had. "My family" did not include Hannah. She was not part of what I considered my new family unit; Hannah was in a new category of in-laws to my wife and part of a different family unit that consisted of my parents and her. All my decisions over the next ten months came back to this internal decision that I was only responsible for and responsible to my new family, which was Katie and Kyle. Looking back, I didn't even treat Hannah like a good roommate, which was the position I had placed her in. I wasn't acting like her brother, and I wasn't acting like a good roommate to Hannah either.

Why was not going to Taco Bell such a big deal to her? After much thought over several years, I realized that it was a simple problem with a simple solution. Hannah wanted me to treat her as an equal, and instead, I was treating her like I was her dad, telling her what to do. I didn't consider her input; I just acted on what was easiest for me, Katie, and Kyle. I could have better communicated my needs to Hannah, or I could have even just sucked it up and gotten her Taco Bell to keep my word to her.

At the time, I couldn't see it. All I could see was my little sister throwing a fit because she didn't get her way, and I dismissed her feelings all together. I began doing that a lot—began labeling all our confrontations as the same problem, one I did not want to deal with. When I would find out later exactly what a borderline person deals with, it broke my heart. Hearing myself speak to her now, knowing how Hannah heard it through the perspective of her Borderline Personality Disorder was crushing. I know my mom tried to explain it to me back then, but it just didn't register.

I regret not understanding Hannah's needs, and I regret that my words harmed her more than I could understand. I regret how I hurt my mother during the Colorado Confrontation, because the day I took out my anger on Hannah in front of her, I forced my mom into silence. She didn't know how to respond to her two adult children fighting, when one of them should have been able to take the high road and didn't. The Colorado Confrontation was our last issue before leaving Colorado, and the trip to Taco Bell was the first. After Taco Bell, the next trial would be Christmas a few weeks later.

I was sitting in the car with my brother complaining about Hannah. I needed someone to vent to who would understand how unreasonable Hannah was being. My brother didn't have much to say, except that he understood my frustration and reminded me to be patient. I should have taken his advice more, seeing that he was the oldest of all five.

If I had a complaint about my one younger sibling, I could only imagine how many complaints he had heard from all of us over the years. One of his strengths that I admire most is his ability to pick and choose his battles, only arguing about things that truly matter. He has been, and continues to be, more than a peacemaker. He is the voice of reason among our group.

His Christmas present that year was to take all of us to see the newest movie with the most technological advancement in years, *Avatar*, in Imax 3D. He bought a ticket for all the siblings and their spouses. He was an electrical engineer in Silicon Valley; who was I to stop his blessing to all of us? I think he has done more than enough to spoil me over the years, so you would think I would have learned to be a better older sibling by his example.

Maybe it was because we were both guys, I'm not sure, but I do know that I did not return in kind this treatment to Hannah during our time in Colorado. Instead, I stood in judgment over all the little things so that when the big things came, they seemed way bigger than they should have. The little thing at the theater that Christmas was the popcorn and soda.

Hannah had asked Alex for some money for popcorn and soda. My brother agreed and told her to get a large for us all to share. The previews had started by the time she returned with the popcorn and drink … or maybe she had just asked for popcorn and added the drink? Maybe she asked for the drink and added the popcorn? The sequencing of questions, and what Hannah purchased, was not the point.

Hannah gladly shared the popcorn, but when someone asked for a drink, she said, "Oh, I'm sick, and it's diet. I don't think you would want any."

I snarked back, "You didn't buy soda to share?"

I heard grumbling from another sibling, and my brother piped in, "Guys, it's not a big deal!"

"But it wasn't her money," I stated emphatically.

My brother could have easily put me in my place by pointing out that it was *his* money. He had purchased the movie tickets, and he didn't care how Hannah spent the money, but he spared me the embarrassment. "Let's just enjoy the movie. It is going to be mind-blowing."

I never saw *Avatar* again after that, even though it made a ton of money and was spectacular in 3D on an Imax screen. My brother explained that James Cameron had created his own patented technology that filmed the movie in 3D instead of just adding it after the fact. This special camera, along with the glasses provided, created a true depth that your eyes could see.

At the end of the movie, everyone was fine, but I couldn't let go of the fact that Hannah had kept the drink all to herself.

"How selfish," I complained to Katie later. "Why does she only do things for herself and mooch off everyone else? Alex had already bought us tickets to the movie, and she had to go and ask for more?"

It reminded me of the Taco Bell day that made her mad. I was always supposed to cater to her needs. I had a three-year-old and a new wife, and a twenty-year-old sister who was not self-sufficient; it was a burden I was not willing to carry. Two incidents in a matter of two weeks meant I would keep a tally of many more.

A friend once joked with me that I had an Excel sheet on my computer where I kept tabs of who I owed money to and who owed money to me. I guess this was an example of me keeping score and holding grudges. I don't forget; I bottle it up. I don't pay back; I stop borrowing. It is pretty one-sided, and when it came to Hannah, I wouldn't forget and would make sure not to let the situation happen again. If it did happen again, I would begin to confront her, and by confronting, I mean I was passive-aggressive.

For Christmas that year, as with years past and the years to come, Hannah made crafts as gifts for everyone. It started as cute and creative, but this Christmas it was a breach of propriety. Hannah had framed photos of our wedding to give to my mom and us—photos she took. I was infuriated. Why would she, without asking, frame photos of *my* wedding and give them as gifts? Didn't she know that we paid a photographer and had professional photos that we planned to use as gifts at our discretion? Who does that? What twenty-year-old take photos of someone else's wedding, prints them, and gives them as a gift to her parents, passing off the idea as if it was her job? In my mind, that is something you do not need to explain to anyone. The photos of someone's weddings are the couple's, and you don't post anything on social media without asking the couple if it is okay.

A lot of weddings nowadays encourage people to post many photos so that the couple can collect them later. The point is still the same, though: the photos are for the couple to use and create memories with and give as gifts. I was baffled that Hannah didn't understand that concept. I recalled that she did it with one of the twins' wedding years before, and I would notice that she did it more in the next couple years with the next two weddings, of the other twin and my brother.

I said something to my mom about my issue with Hannah's gifts; I don't think I said anything to Hannah though, because I was so bothered by it. My mom said Hannah didn't have any money, and this was her way of showing us honor.

"Mom," I stated, "those are not her pictures to give away. Why is she making gifts with something that isn't hers to give?"

My mother always assumed the best in someone's intentions with all of us children. "She didn't mean to step on your toes, Matt Jo. She doesn't have much to give," Mom replied. It was the third strike, and we had only been in Colorado for three weeks.

I remember that Katie loaned Hannah some of her movies and wanted one of them back. I marched up to Hannah's room and made a big deal out of nothing. My wife was voicing a frustration, not wanting me to fix it, but it was my sister, and Hannah had crossed a boundary: don't borrow our stuff and not return it.

When I went up to Hannah's room, I noticed another movies of ours. I made another big deal out of it, which ended with Hannah crying because I told her she couldn't borrow our movies anymore. I'm positive I was not tactful or graceful, just blunt. I think what upset me about her borrowing them was that she didn't take care of the DVDs. She just left them on her shelf, piled them up after she watched each one, and didn't put them back in the case. I felt it was common courtesy to put movies back in the case so they don't get scratched.

DVD displacement would be a problem with our children—no child puts a DVD back—and I remedied the problem of having a thousand DVDs laying around. I took an old CD case Katie had and put every single movie and game in this giant zip-up binder. It was perfect for all our road trips and easy for the kids to access and return.

Obviously, I had a pet peeve about DVDs getting scratched, and for Hannah to borrow them, she needed to follow my rules. I suppose I had a lot of rules I placed upon her. I think I was difficult to live with. As I said, I was not a good roommate.

On another occasion—one she brought up multiple times—Hannah wanted music from my iTunes on my laptop. She came down to the basement and said, "Hey, can you put your music on my iPod?"

"No," I replied.

Hannah was a bit caught off guard and asked why.

I replied, "It's Katie's and my music, and I don't feel right just giving all of it to you."

She responded, "We share music all the time. What's the difference?"

I thought about it, and she was right—up until our move to Colorado, we would exchange music. I would make her a copy of my things, and I would make copies of hers. Trading CDs was one thing, but asking for my entire music library seemed a bit much. I held my ground and explained that I could make her a specific CD, which was our usual arrangement. However, I did not want simply to give her all my music.

Music had been our shared love, something that deeply connected us since Hannah's teenage years. She had introduced me to a lot of music I liked that still reminds me of her today. I thought my response was fair, and I still would not give someone my entire music library today. I don't know how I could have responded better at that moment; possibly just saying no was not the tact that was needed.

When a person holds a grudge, everything that comes out of the mouth has a pointed edge. It may be a true statement or a healthy boundary, but the heart's position in a grudge makes the words sting. I shut the door on one of the key places where Hannah and I had connected for the previous five or six years of her life, and I would not allow any negotiating. I believe Hannah was hurt that I made a boundary that music would not be our thing anymore. Through all our traveling, there was a lot of emotional traversing that occurred where I did not care how it might impact my sister.

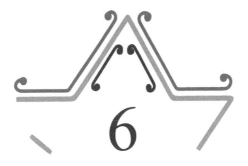

6

Road Trips and Concerts

When I was in college and Hannah was in high school, we shared the same taste in music, and that remained true. I would give her copies of my CDs, and she would give me copies of hers. Some of the best memories I have with my sister center around our love for music.

My freshman year of college, my parents asked if I would take Hannah and her friend to a Relient K and Anberlin concert that was out of town. They would even let me take their new Honda CRV. It was a win-win. I wanted more independence, since I hadn't left town for college, and they didn't have the energy to drive so late into the evening.

Driving out of town was a big deal for me, because I wasn't allowed to in high school. Part of my mom and stepdad showing me that they now viewed me as an adult, based on a counselor's suggestion, was that I have some independence to drive out of town. They listened to the counselor's advice and set up something even better: a road trip with my sister and her crazy friend jamming out to music. I picked up Hannah and her friend from school; it was a check on the cool factor for me to be picking her up at school instead of mom. All their friends were jealous that Hannah's older brother, who was in college, was taking them to a Relient K concert.

On our way to the venue, we had dinner at In-N-Out, the staple of every road trip, then went and got in line for the concert. We even got the lead singer's autograph, though I'm not sure how we managed to run into him. "M@" was how he signed his name, and I wished I was a rock star so that I could think of something as clever as that. "M@ JO" could still work, I suppose.

At this concert, I learned the lesson that wearing hearing aids at a rock concert was not a good idea when everyone starts jumping up and down. My right hearing aid popped out of my ear. I told Hannah and her friend, and we tried to find it—to no avail. I told them it was not a big deal, and we kept dancing the night away.

Two Lefts Don't Make a Right, But Three Do was the band's newest album, and the band played all of Hannah's favorite songs, and even the one I was hoping to hear: "I Am Understood." It was my rock anthem, a cry out to God wanting, hoping, and wishing I could accept His forgiveness. Relient K was an edgy Christian group in their early days. Their less overtly Christian songs were playing in both youth groups and secular spaces across the nation. "I Am Understood" was one of those songs that had a double meaning. Hannah and I had that in common—liking these sort of songs the most. We both had a deep desire to be heard, to be seen, to be loved, and to be understood. I understood Hannah back then. I understood her needs and met them in every way I could as an older brother.

The concerts we attended usually centered around the bands she enjoyed and that I grew to enjoy. Another concert date with the same friend was at a church in Prescott; it was a Kutless concert featuring Thousand Foot Krutch and a new band called FM Static. I knew Kutless well, and Hannah and her friend loved Thousand Foot Krutch, a very heavy rock band. The music involved loud screaming that I didn't particularly like at times but grew to appreciate. That concert was fun because the band FM Static opened, and their music was poppy but catchy. It would be a band that Hannah and I would often listen to together. We listened to "Crazy Mary" all the way home that night.

After FM Static left the stage, Thousand Foot Krutch came out, and I looked at Hannah and said, "Isn't that the same guy? He just took his hat off and changed clothes?"

I was confused. Can a guy do that—play in two different bands at the same concert? He didn't say anything, he just flipped from pop rock to heavy rock in a matter of fifteen minutes and pretended like nothing was different.

My favorite part of our concert road trips was the evening drives home. I would find a gas station to fill up the tank and get myself a soda, and my sister and her friend would fall asleep in the back after their music high wore off. Then it was just me and the open road. If the moon was out, I could see the hillsides chase me around every turn as the horizon moved up and down. My parents gave me responsibility that I perceived as independence, which satisfied my desire to be treated no longer as a child.

There would be many trips during my years in college. We would make several more trips to Phoenix, a trip to Prescott, and an even bigger trip to California on two separate occasions to go to Spirit West Coast, the largest summer Christian music festival on the west coast at the time. Many trips carried specific memories. One of the concerts we went to was at an outdoor venue, and even though no one cared for the opening band, Hannah and I were the first ones to run up to the stage. Our game plan was to wait out the beginning bands so that we could be there for the big ones.

This specific concert was with Audio Adrenaline as one of the lead bands, and later Michael W. Smith, a singer I have loved since I was a child. During one of Audio Adrenaline's ending songs, they invited people from the crowd up onto the stage. I screamed at the top of my lungs and waved my hands in the air, and Hannah did the same but pointed at me. She would have been mortified to be up in front of all those people, but she knew I would do it in a heartbeat.

Mark Stuart, the lead singer, grabbed my hand and pulled me up onstage. I don't remember the song, but I remember going crazy, jumping up and down to whatever motions Mark gave us. It was one of those "I'm never washing this hand again" moments but ten times cooler, because I got in a quick hug at the end. If you ever sing "Big House" at church camp, you have this band to think.

Taking Hannah to concerts was somewhat in our family DNA. These concerts were unforgettable growing up because my family didn't have a ton of money with five children in the house. There were only a handful of extravagant events in our household. Birthdays were one, because we would get Peter Piper Pizza, always. It was the only time we ordered out. However, the main thing my parents decided when we were younger was to take us to see concerts, even before Hannah was old enough to join us. My parents allowing me to take her to concerts was their way of passing on the torch to me.

My experience of jumping onstage with Audio Adrenaline was a decade in the making. It was bound to happen. We'd paid our dues. One of us had to have our five seconds of fame, and Hannah witnessed this glorious moment and spectacle.

"Matt Jo, that was so awesome!" she yelled and high-fived me as I got off the stage. I thanked her for screaming for me. Out of all the concerts I have been to, that moment was the highlight of them all—not my number-one concert but my favorite moment at any concert.

The other major trip I remember my parents letting Hannah and I take—and I'm still unclear as to why my parents trusted me so much—was a driving trip with Hannah to California to go to Spirit West Coast in Del Mar. We bought the tickets for the whole event, a three-day pass. It was just the two of us, walking around from concert to concert. I don't remember the evening headliners; I don't remember anything unusual, except, of course, seeing Relient K. What I do remember was waking up on that Saturday morning, both of us exhausted from all the new territory we had traversed. We decided to be lazy in the hotel room and watch cartoons.

There was a marathon of this show that was trying to be as cool as Pokemon was. It was called *Digimon: Digital Monsters*. It was another thing we had in common: we were both content with doing nothing, watching TV, and watching something as silly as a Japanese children's cartoon. Hannah knew all about it and explained the show to me as we watched it. That was probably the most fun adult decision we made—realizing we could get up and go whenever we wanted to because no one was telling us where we had to be and at what time. We just did our own thing.

The other major part of this adventure was me driving and Hannah helping me navigate the crazy Southern California highways and traffic. We made it to the festival, to the hotel, back and forth a couple more times, and then back home. It was a needed vacation for both of us, and I think my parents were happy to provide us with the money to take it. My mom gave me a lot of responsibility. Hearing the words, "I trust you" is huge. Hannah wanted to go to concerts, and I wanted the responsibility. Hannah enjoyed my company, and I enjoyed hers.

I had a specific reason back then for why I invested so much time into my relationship with Hannah. When she was fourteen and I was in my first year of college, my mom and stepdad admitted her into the behavioral health unit at the city hospital. I was a youth leader volunteer at my church, and she was one of the middle-school students. My mom called me and told me what had happened. She and my stepdad had been concerned about Hannah's mental health for some time. Hannah finally admitted to my parents that she "didn't want to live anymore." My parents made a very brave decision to have her admitted into the hospital's behavioral health ward, where they would keep a close watch on her for forty-eight hours.

I cried when my mom told me how Hannah was feeling. I'd had my battles with depression, but never to the point of feeling suicidal. I had been involved for a little over a year as a youth leader at our church, and my calling to work with teenagers was beginning to stir within me. I remember going to see her during visiting hours that same day. I hugged her and cried and told her how much I loved her. I didn't have much advice, as I knew she just wanted my presence.

For some reason, I told her that I would love to help her clean her room, that sometimes when we feel out of control on the inside, it helps to find something we can control. Organizing one's surroundings can provide relief from the anxiety that clutter brings. The reason I offered this was that I had just moved out of the house, and I felt partly responsible for her misery. I know there were so many other things going on in her, but being the youngest of five and the last one at home couldn't be easy. Since I was not in the house, Hannah had the freedom to be in whatever room she wanted—a fresh start since everything had changed.

At the hospital, I committed to being a better big brother to her and loving and helping her through her teenage years. I took flowers to her on her birthday one year at school to surprise her. I went to movie premieres with her, waited in line, ate popcorn and drank soda in line, and then got our free refill once the movie started. Growing up, I remember seeing two movies in the theater with my whole family: *Aladdin* and *Back to the Future 3*. When we got older, and it was just Hannah at home, my parents paid for us to see any blockbuster movie that came out.

My first car died in the Harkins Theatres parking lot on one of those movie outings. It was a memorable moment watching that car try to sputter itself back to life as Hannah chuckled that I cared too much about my antique 1984 Toyota Tercel. It had been my brother's first and then mine, and the best part about it was that he had put in a CD player with an amp under the driver's seat and ten-inch bass speakers in the back. I felt cool driving the "egg," as his friends called it.

Even more importantly, 1984 was the year I was born. Maybe every teenager's first car should be from the year they were born so that they can appreciate a good car when they get one. Hannah would have her fair share of beat-up cars to drive, but sadly, the egg would not be one of them.

I wanted to leave town for college, but my mother insisted I stay since I had tuition covered and my older siblings were attending the same university. Traversing the territory of a university can be challenging, and my mom had already helped three of her children navigate the waters of admissions and the ins and outs of financial aid and the option to live at home if needed. At some point early in Hannah's time in high school and my time in college, Hannah started cutting herself, and her depression seemed to worsen. Hannah did not tell anyone about it and kept it a secret to deal with her pain.

The summer after my first year in college, I got an internship at a church in Northern California. This was the big opportunity for me; I was going to finally get my moment away from the small town in which I had grown up and have an important college experience going to an unknown place on my own for the first time. It was during this summer I was gone that Hannah finally experienced the freedom of releasing her secret.

Losing a marriage will always be a fear of mine for my parents. One life-altering straw that statistically shatters the vertebrae of the proverbial camel in marriage is the death of a child. If all else is not in place or as it should be in a marriage, this event will tear it apart. Since Hannah's death, and learning of this possibility with my parents, I started to worry about my own marriage. What if the worst happened? What if one of our children died?

My mom used to pray, "God, if one of my children dies, may it not be my fault, and may they know you." I wish I could say God answered my mom's prayer, but as the events unfolded surrounding Hannah's passing, she could not help but blame herself as any parent would.

To have your flesh and blood lay dying or dead at your feet when it seems preventable is the epitome of despair. Cancer, car accidents, catastrophic acts of God are unavoidable, but Hannah's passing was not one of those. It was not black or white, with no clear line or definitive motive. Everything about her death seemed like one big cosmic accident, if one believes in such a thing. How can we ask the dead the true motive behind the choices that led to their demise?

Whether directly or indirectly—stepping behind the wheel drunk or being unaware of how many toxins your body can handle—the motive behind death is a guess.

My own thoughts about Hannah's death are more definitive, but they also definitively change from year to year. My pain and regret may increase or decrease depending on how I interpret her motives. Was her choice of ingesting too much of a prescribed narcotic intentional, or did she not know how much to take? Did she intentionally mix different medications, or was she trying to just compensate the upper with a downer? Why did she take the risk to begin with? These answers would become clearer as the investigation into her death came to a close.

Anyone who tells you they know something without any doubt is only fooling themselves. Whether one is an atheist or a devout Christian, there is always a place where belief meets doubt and faith bridges the gap. There are no absolute answers about life after death apart from faith. We can't ask the dead, and we won't know until we get there ourselves.

When I think about death, I remember the classic riddle, "The man who built it does not keep it, the man who bought it does not use it, and the man who uses it does not know it. What is it?" Well, we had to buy one: Hannah's final resting place, a simple wooden box. One of the saddest sounds is the final closing of a casket and the locking mechanism that ensures it does not open again. It is a forced goodbye.

It wasn't that Hannah's funeral was not set up to say goodbye, it was just that the locking of her coffin meant we would never see Hannah's face again. I regret looking at her post-embalming, and I regret that I couldn't be at peace with it. I regret that I did not feel sad when I heard the locking sound, as the rest of my family did. Instead, I was glad to move on. The waiting period between her death and funeral was the worst part, and I had already said goodbye several times.

While my siblings wailed and cried at the sound of her casket closing, I was a little relieved, but I would never dare share that. I've come to realize I'm not designed to be a person who must deal with decaying bodies. Doctors, caregivers, and morticians have a unique calling of walking among the dead, and I do not share it.

Hannah had just finished her freshman year in high school the summer I was gone interning in California. She went to summer camp with my home church while I was away—the same camp that I grew up going to. The first time I had a "mountaintop experience" was at that same camp. Every summer I would go to this high school camp and have my "come to Jesus" moment, and then I would return home to be challenged by the monotony of everyday life. A week of loud music, amazing speakers, reading the Bible, being encouraged to pursue Jesus, and feeling like it's possible to accept his grace daily was easily drowned out by the pressures of the teenage life.

The constant battle to chase the feeling that was once there but slowly distanced itself is spiritually draining, especially when you're around friends who don't believe what you believe. Nevertheless, this perceived feeling that God is right next to you, holding you, and loving you because you had come clean of the sin in your life was palpable. Then the work mentality begins because you equate the mountaintop feeling to the work of not sinning; if you could only stop sinning, you could gain that feeling back. I struggled with whether camp as a teenager was helpful or was doing some psychological damage by creating this illusion that God is only there at certain times and in certain places. My summer in California showed me that it is possible to take God with you—or more importantly, that you can leave open the eyes of your soul and see that God is always there.

Hannah called me in California in the middle of her week at camp. She called me in tears to tell me she had given her life to Jesus and felt whole for the first time. I cried with her, remembering the same experience I'd had with Jesus. I was encouraged to see Hannah come out of the depths of her despair and wanting to die, to finding her life in how Jesus viewed her no matter what she had done. If I had not been working at this church up in Northern Calfornia and having my own experience with Jesus, I probably would have been cynical about Hannah's experience. I knew life would be just as hard upon her return as it was before she left for camp. Instead, I think God had placed us in the same moment, at the same time, to be an encouragement to each other.

One of my worries about going to California was leaving my sister, and now I had news of hopefulness, that she was ready to try again. The conclusion I came to about summer camp with teenagers—which I had to because I eventually became a youth pastor—was, if not a summer camp experience, what else? What hope do we have for teenagers if not to pull them out of their normal daily routine and allow them to hear God without all the clutter? At least they know what it sounds like when Jesus woos you and softens your heart. Scripture says, "Since we live by the Spirit, let us keep in step with the Spirit" (Galatians 5:25).

Sometimes it is a feeling, and sometimes it requires work, but the reality is that none of this is the basis for our salvation. All of this happens after we have been justified by faith in Christ. Becoming like him is the hard part. We often mistake our sin as a sign that we do not have salvation. We think we cannot sense God's presence as we once did in an environment where we can hear his calling. Feelings come and go, but our salvation is secure, and it is our *sanctification* that occurs when we work on overcoming our sinful nature by the power of the Spirit.

Even deeper to the heart of our transformation into the likeness of Jesus is that it is the Spirit working inside of us, done by faith as well.

We are saved by faith and transformed by that very same faith. This level of thinking took me years of growth; it took going to seminary to fix some bad theology. It took becoming a high school Bible teacher of the New Testament Epistles to understand what the authors were truly saying, not just what other people said they were saying.

This ebb and flow of feeling and not feeling God, working for God's grace and then just accepting it, is what would play out for Hannah over the next ten years of her life. It would take Hannah a decade to learn that God is always there, had always loved her, and had picked up her broken heart and given her a new one. She would come to understand that she had a calling, a purpose, a plan for her life. It started for Hannah that summer at camp, but the pain to come in those moments appeared unbearable to her and her parents. However, Hannah would get there—to her purpose on this earth—and find her joy before God took her home. God took Hannah from this earth at just the right time, not when she was down in the ditches of misery and sin but after she had weathered the storm of her teenage years, her unforgiving sibling, her diagnosis of Borderline Personality Disorder, and her life of drugs and alcohol.

The next ten years were the hardest and most painful of her life. Was Hannah's time at camp that summer a waste? Was it a bait and switch, setting her up for disappointment? Hope is what Hannah found, and I think her life would have been worse without that summer camp experience. We were both changed for the better, and that camp experience prepared us for the oncoming storms of life. For Hannah, she was changed for her time of living; but for me, it would be the times after her death in which I would change the most, and the things God had been preparing me for would come to fruition when Hannah's soul departed this life as she took her last breath.

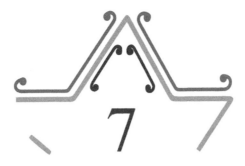

7

The Colorado Confrontation

Our first and only Christmas on Stone Fence Drive had passed. I was well into my first semester at Denver Seminary, driving up Interstate 25 twice a week for my three on-campus classes. While I loved all the Bible portions of things I was learning, it was the degree that I had chosen that felt unsettling. I wanted a two-year program, and we did not want to live in the Denver area.

Toward the end of that semester, right around Hannah's twenty-first birthday, I had come to an impasse with our choice to move to Colorado. If I wanted to change my degree program, it would extend our time, and we would have to move closer to campus. The only way it would work would be to move closer to Littleton, with no family nearby, and start paying for rent.

The other factor weighing on me was my relationship with Hannah. I clearly did not have a lot of positive moments with her during our stay on Stone Fence Drive, but her twenty-first birthday was fun. My mom and stepdad took us all out to eat; we laughed and played games with her that night. It was my stepdad's birthday as well, it was something she looked forward to every year. They would sing, *Happy Birthday to Us* as their tradition. It was a night to focus on her and celebrate her. It is the only distinct memory of fun I had with Hannah during our time on Stone Fence Drive.

Outside of that night, I was bitter toward Hannah. I was holding a grudge from the wedding fall-out, and unable to reconcile it. All the little things just added up. Hannah was selfish and somewhat narcissistic. If she didn't get her way, Hannah would pout or storm off angry. It wasn't just with me; she behaved this way with my parents, and I became defensive for them. Why was their twenty-one-year-old daughter treating them like she was still a teenager? Hannah expected money from them, and even then, she would go over her spending budget and apologize after the fact. Hannah couldn't hold a job and always had a reason for why her jobs didn't work out. Of course, it was never her fault.

Hannah tried to go to the community college for a few semesters, but one math teacher made her feel dumb, so she stopped going. I get that math wasn't Hannah's strength, and we all have professors we don't like, but quitting because of one mean teacher seemed a little extreme. There was always an excuse with Hannah, and between the time I last lived with her at fourteen and now, she had not changed at all. I expected her to have matured to an age-appropriate person, and she hadn't.

Hannah was still completely dependent on my mom and her dad, my stepdad. My mom informed me at different points in our stay how much Hannah had gone through and that she was doing better. Within our first month of being there, Hannah called a family meeting which included Katie, and she gave a box to my stepdad with her marijuana paraphernalia. She said she had been doing drugs again and wanted to stop. My mom informed me of her struggles the past several years before we arrived. Hannah would sneak out often at night and not come back until the next day. She told my parents that she was sexually active; I'm not exactly sure of the details, as it wasn't my business.

There was a lot to take in about Hannah's time in the house on Stone Fence Drive that I didn't learn about until I moved in, and even more after we eventually moved out. When Hannah shared with us about her drug use, I remember being a little shocked, because at that time I didn't know everything that had transpired since they'd had left our hometown when Hannah was sixteen to provide a hopefully better environment for Hannah.

Back in the summer after my freshman year in college, my parents brought Hannah up to Spirit West Coast in Monterey, near where I was doing my internship. It was the same music festival company that Hannah and I had been to before. It was a similar three-day outdoor venue with major artists playing on the main stage each night. I was excited to see Hannah and hang out with my brother and my mom and stepdad.

My mom and stepdad had been talking about moving away from our hometown, partly for my stepdad to find another job, but at the concert, they both felt God telling them they needed to move for Hannah. She was sixteen, in the middle of high school, and her emotional issues were more than most teenagers her age. I remember one of the other leaders at our church telling me that Hannah was just too emotional. It ticked me off, because they didn't even know Hannah or what her struggles were.

My mom has often told me of the perception people had of Hannah as too emotional, even in grade school. It was in the middle of her elementary school years when Hannah complained that her teacher wasn't helping her enough to understand her math. My mom had a meeting, with Hannah and her teacher, and the teacher told Hannah something like, "You are just expecting me to do everything. You want the best cereal, Frosted Flakes that no one else has. You need to be grateful with the Cheerios that everyone gets."

Hannah, in her young wisdom, retorted back in tears, "How could I be asking for better cereal when you haven't even given me a bowl, a spoon, or even milk?"

Hannah knew where she was lacking and knew where she needed help, but for some reason, everyone on the outside saw her as emotional. Hannah was emotional, but developmentally, a lot of people are emotional. With Hannah, I don't think she could control her tears. They would just come. I'm not sure when I stopped seeing her tears as genuine, and I became part of the crowd of people who blamed her for being "too emotional."

My parents and sister moving was another event that I wasn't ready for. My stepdad had already put in a two-week notice at his job and found a new one in Colorado Springs, or ColoSpgs as my mom would call it from the highway signs. My cousin—my mom's niece, who was grown and married with two baby girls of her own—was living in the Springs, which is what the rest of us called it. Her family had a basement for my stepdad and eventually my mom and Hannah to live in. All houses in the Springs had basements.

I guess this was a little foreshadowing of why my parents were okay with allowing my family to live in their basement down the road. They were passing on the grace shown to them in their time of need.

After that first spring semester living in Colorado, I was disheartened that the seminary program I chose was not giving me the ministry training I was looking for. If I switched to a different program, I would have to add more years to our stay in Colorado. In one of my classes I was talking about the theories of youth ministry, when I had just left a youth ministry position where I was living out these theories. This drove me crazy, why did God have me leave a job, only to find out that I was doing it right and didn't need this specific program. I decided to switch to a different seminary that had more online options, study part-time and find a full-time youth ministry position. Our reason for being in Colorado had come to an end.

In this decision making process I realized there was no way I could live in the house on Stone Fence Drive another semester anyways.

My relationship with Hannah couldn't handle it; it would break, and it would not be healthy for me, her, my wife, or my son. I saw it as an impossibility, something unfixable.

It was summer, our time was flexible, and we hadn't told my parents our plans to find a place of our own and move out. I knew the longer I stayed on Stone Fence Drive, the more my relationship with Hannah would deteriorate past what it had, and it would deteriorate within the coming months as the Colorado Confrontation approached. I don't think I realized how much we were asking of my parents to watch Kyle, and I didn't recognize how much Hannah watched Kyle during the first month of Katie working and when I started a temporary job while I waited for a youth ministry position to open up.

Hannah babysitting Kyle was the breaking point of tension between us. It kicked off the argument that broke us, the confrontation that severed an already tender relationship. Hannah needed recognition for watching Kyle, and I withheld that from her, intentionally.

For a long time, I would regret my time in Colorado. I felt that the cost of my time, energy, money invested in school—which was a transaction into debt—and of course my tumultuous relationship with Hannah was not worth the cost. A semester in school and moving to and from Colorado seemed like wasted physical exertion. I questioned God a lot, thinking I had missed some big sign from the universe or that it was some sort of test, a time of wandering in the desert for something I had done wrong, only to return to where I had started. Things started looking better when I had an actual job offer on the table to work as a youth pastor, but in a different state.

My stepdad said, "It sounds like a natural fit. You have a young family, and providing for them is your priority."

I wasn't sure how to break the news to Hannah that we were moving away. It would hurt her, but I wasn't sure I was the one to tell her, since I hadn't been very sensitive to her needs. My parents eventually did, and she told Katie and me that she was sad but understood our need to go.

Katie and I had a date set for when we would pack up and leave. It was going to be the end of August, but I ended up moving our departure earlier by two weeks. This decision was the moment I would live to regret for years to come, and even more after Hannah's passing.

The Colorado Confrontation was how our time in Colorado ended. At the time, I justified everything I was saying. I was standing up for my wife and child. It wasn't until years later when I read what exactly a BPD is that I understood the problem. Everything a borderline person struggles with is what I fed to Hannah that day and fueled her disorder.

The main concern of a person with BPD is abandonment. People with this disorder have an irrational fear that people will abandon them, even to the point of setting up situations where the person with BPD is very difficult to love. They will push you away and then blame you for abandoning them.

I ended up doing was this very thing, but it was worse because she *didn't* push me away, I intentionally abandoned her, knowing that it would hurt her in some way. It is one thing for people with BPD to push a loved one away, but when that loved one really does abandon them, it is soul-crushing. I knew what abandonment felt like from when my family had moved to Colorado, and it was the one thing I knew would show I had the upper hand. It was a revenge tactic. She hurt me, so I passively but intentionally hurt her back.

The day of the Colorado Confrontation, my wife and I went to a marriage conference, and my mom volunteered to babysit. What transpired while we were at this conference was that my mom voiced frustration in front of Hannah about how we were gone longer than she expected us to be. On our way back home, we were maybe ten minutes away, I got a text from Hannah asking, "Where are you? Mom and I have been waiting for you for a long time?"

I was dumbfounded as I read the text. I don't think I was driving, because my blood was boiling as I thought of what I needed to say back. My sister had the nerve to butt into a situation that had absolutely nothing to do with her. How dare she get into the middle of something that was between my mother and I and instigate a problem that wasn't necessary? If my mom had a problem with our tardiness or lack of communication, she could tell me herself. I didn't need my little sister speaking to me on her behalf.

I texted back, "I didn't know you were babysitting. I thought Mom was."

She retorted, "We both are. That's how we work. We both babysit Kyle when you leave."

Who does she think she is? I thought to myself. I never asked her to babysit and never agreed to this shared babysitting responsibility. I did not appreciate her confronting me on behalf of my mom, who was a grown woman and could confront me herself. This was the last straw. I couldn't handle this from Hannah anymore. She was messing with my life, my marriage, and my parenting on every level, and I'd had enough. I was going to confront her and lay it all out on the table—air out all my grievances.

I wanted to hurl the past ten months of frustration at her one stabbing word at a time. I knew I couldn't confront her by myself—it would be her word against mine—and I couldn't drag Katie into it because it wasn't her sister or her problem. It was my problem, and I needed to handle it, so I asked my mom to sit in on my conversation with Hannah.

We pulled up to the house, and I told Katie that once we got there, she should take Kyle and head down to the basement. I asked my mom and Hannah if we could talk in the living room, and they both agreed. I told my mom that I wanted her there so that she could be the third person in the room to hear our conversation.

I started with my first problem, which was, "Why was it your business to text me that we were late?"

Hannah responded that she and Mom had been waiting for over an hour and had not heard from us.

I felt like I repeated five times in that conversation these exact words: "I never asked you to babysit Kyle." I felt like I needed to pummel her into submission. She was butting her nose into my business, and it had nothing to do with her. "If Mom is upset, Mom can tell me, and I don't need you to tell me for Mom," I exclaimed.

I had noticed this behavior between my mom and stepdad: Hannah would step into the middle of one of their arguments, trying to take sides and help end the argument. It was a point of frustration for me that they would allow her to insert herself the way she did.

I don't remember everything she said or everything I said in those twenty minutes, but I know I made myself clear: she was not to speak to me on behalf of Mom. I didn't ask; I demanded it.

Then came the kicker, the knife that I drove into her heart. They were words I could never take back; words that built up a barrier in our relationship to sever it; words that created a boundary she had to stay within because it wasn't safe next to me; words that were intended to point out an obvious truth but were said without any form of love; words void of any form of brotherly affection toward my sister; words that had been hiding for a long time about the truth of how I viewed her. "Hannah," I said, "you can't be the victim all the time."

Silence filled the room. I looked over at my mom. She was wide-eyed, and her mouth was almost frowning. I couldn't interpret her feelings. I assumed that she would say something to stop me or defend Hannah, but she said nothing. Her silence I took as neutral, so I continued my assault until I felt I had made my point.

"Don't butt into our business. Don't speak for Mom, and don't get upset with me if I haven't specifically asked you to babysit."

Sobbing, Hanna nodded and said, "Fine."

I walked away and went down to the basement. I was still fuming, and I felt like I had to get out of that house. I told Katie we should take

Kyle to the mall to let him run off some energy. Then I vented as Katie listened. I forced her to take sides simply by venting. Looking back, it was unfair to put Katie in the middle of my relationship with Hannah when they had one of their own.

I had not realized what was happening every day when I was at school or studying. Katie would take Kyle to the library, out to eat, or out to play, and Hannah would be right there with her. Hannah and Katie had spent many hours bonding, many of them over books. *Twilight, Hunger Games,* and *Divergent* were a few among the hundred books they both read that year. Hannah didn't like all the content in adult novels, so she stuck to the teen section to find her books. Katie liked Hannah's strategy and found some of her own favorite books, outside of books written from other mothers and bloggers. These were books written for entertainment, imagination, and love, but they left out the derogatory material in adult books.

Katie did a good job of being peacemaker, and I was grateful for it. She would listen to me and would continue in her friendship with Hannah, never to talk about me with her.

When we were at the mall that same day, I made a decision that was meant to hide my true intentions. "Let's move now," I said to Katie. Why wait until the end of the month? My real reason for leaving was to get away from Hannah. If ever there was a time I was abandoning my sister, this was it. I felt I had no choice; I was only going to get more upset with her.

I never told Hannah or my parents my real reason for moving two weeks sooner than we had intended. It was my way of getting back at her. I couldn't control her, but I could control my family's interactions with her, and I knew that if I left, I would be taking Katie and Kyle away from her too. It would be my lasting message that she should have minded her own business when warned. I didn't have to stick around and put up with her immature attitude and behavior.

Not only was I taking my family away from her, but I was also doing it spontaneously and suddenly. By the time we had packed everything and were ready to go, I don't even remember saying goodbye to her. I know she cried; her closest friend was Katie, and the boy she loved the most was going away. My justification? *That's what you get when you can't respect other people's boundaries. People don't want to be around you,* I thought to myself.

I was on the warpath, packing up all our belongings within days, renting a truck, and filling it up. The church where I was hired at was reimbursing our moving expenses, so money wasn't an issue at all. I was leaving because I wanted to abandon Hannah—to leave her to herself and not look back. Years later, when I learned that this was the greatest fear of someone with BPD, I cried. If there was anyone who didn't deserve to be abandond, it was my sister.

Anger can cloud judgment and empathy. It makes wise men fools and good men stumble. Unrestrained anger is not from God. Anger is not a sin, but when it lacks self-control, it manifests itself in very unholy and selfish ways that are sinful. Revenge was the form my anger had taken in me, and Hannah received the brute end of my attack. I felt that it was my job to make sure that she understood she had crossed the line. She found ways to not take the blame for things, it seemed impossible to confront her. There was no fixing a problem.

I also would not allow her to get in the middle of my affairs, which didn't concern her. It was as if she had become my enemy and was no longer my sister. I was very protective of my boundary, and there was no option to negotiate because I didn't give her one.

I know now that what I said crushed Hannah's spirit. She was crushed by her brother who had invested so much time in her life as a teenager—her brother who drove her to California for concerts, her brother who flew out to the Springs for her eighteenth birthday to surprise her, her brother who had been looking out for her. I had turned against her, and I was proud of it. In my arrogance, I thought I had done what was necessary to stand up for myself and the needs of my family.

I did not respond to Hannah appropriately that day. I allowed months of bottled-up emotion to build to a point where an explosion was inevitable. All she did was send me a text implying my mom was tired of waiting for Katie and me to return home to get Kyle. I could have asked my mom or simply apologized to my mom for not communicating better and approach Hannah at a different time. I could have thanked Hannah for letting me know how mom was feeling. There were so many things I could have done differently. I regret not choosing something different. I regret not taking a moment to myself before I walked in the house. I regret not deciding that this was not worth risking my relationship with Hannah.

My mom's advice has always been to "apologize even if you didn't do anything wrong." An apology upfront will always diffuse a situation. My mom didn't mean it needed to be insincere or fake but to legitimately find something you can own up to in a conflict, even if it was an admission that something went wrong or that you could have responded better. All this to say, I knowingly went after my sister with the intention of getting her to submit to me as the older sibling. I wanted complete control of our relationship for fear that she would inadvertently make a decision that would cause harm to me, either directly or indirectly. I wanted to keep her at a distance. The last choice I would make that day was to move sooner rather than later, which was a weapon I aimed, with Hannah in my crosshairs.

It is amazing the strength you find when you are determined to do something. We said our goodbyes to my mom, stepdad, and Hannah, and we were off to start our family journey solo, just the three of us. As quickly as we had whirled into Hannah's life in the Springs, we rolled out. It never occurred to me, even with the pain I left her in, that she was caused more pain by not having anyone around—not having Kyle to interact with, not having Katie to read books with, not having her to watch TV shows and movies with. I removed my family from her quickly because deep down, I knew that would make a lasting impression on her.

I don't know to what extent of depression she sank into after we left, but I do know it was familiar to her. She was depressed before we got there. I'm not sure I cared about her depression as I once had after we left. Once she became an adult, or not a teenager anymore, I just expected her to deal with life the way I had to. I expected the impossible from her, a person who had BPD. She could not respond to me at the level of reasonableness that comes from other young adults. The way her brain perceived the reality around her was flawed, and because of my lack of understanding about her disorder, I was unable to be the brother I once was. There wasn't a way she could have "won me over," because I had shut her out.

I needed to move on from Stone Fence Drive and not look back. In the back of my mind, living with my sister was a mistake, and I blamed all my problems on that. I blamed her for my frustrations while living in Colorado, and I blamed her for why we needed to leave. I would carry a lot of regret, guilt, and shame with me after Hannah's death. These feelings would be revisited at several points in the years after, as I learned more about her disorder and realized both how wrong I was and how I had missed an opportunity to speak the truth in love to her. I didn't see it in the moment of leaving, but what they say is true: hindsight is 20/20.

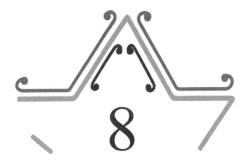

8

There and Back Again

After the Colorado Confrontation and the move back to my home state, my contact with Hannah was minimal. It would be several years before we were living close to them again. In the years after we left the basement on Stone Fence Drive, Katie and I would have time to focus on growing our own family. Having a house to ourselves for the first time finally gave us the independence and family unity we needed. I was finding fulfillment in my youth pastor career, I continued my education through Fuller Seminary and Katie was raising babies. Levi came next during this time, the students in my ministry got to watch Levi grow from a baby to a toddler and would look out for our boys as they hung around on some of our late ministry nights.

There is a lot of work that goes into working with teenagers, many theories, and a twisted theology crept into my actions. "Pursue the students who are leaders," I was told. Those leaders will then attract more students.

Hannah was able to recognize the type of people who played favorites immediately—probably because, like me, she was not always chosen to be part of any selective groups. Hannah didn't even have the benefit of siblings of a similar age going into high school. Not sharing the same last name and having the rest of us off at college created a separation from the members of the Diaz clan who had preceded her. No one knew who the Zellers were.

Hannah did not get picked for teams. When teachers called out names from a roster, she was always last, and she hated it. When you are like Hannah and feel left out a lot, you can easily identify the people on the other side who are doing the choosing. Favoritism hurt her. It hurts everyone, and it is especially painful inside the church. When people who are supposed to represent God leave out others, those left out feel God is rejecting them. Hannah felt this at school and at church. She had some good leaders who would invest in her, but as she entered high school, her new leaders invested time in the popular girls.

This was the twisted theology I was taught: if you invest in students who are "leaders," then you are building God's kingdom, because those perceived leaders would lead their peers to youth group. The whole problem with this mentality is that the students we labeled as "leaders" were always the popular kids. The basis for popularity is selection by a larger group of peers for mostly superficial reasons. To structure a church ministry recruiting model on the consensus of teenager opinion is ludicrous. Where are the adults in the room if we emotionally sink to our teenage years and allow that to guide who we invest time in? It's the blind leading the blind if youth pastors and volunteer leaders pick and choose popular kids.

Also, assuming that popular kids will attract large groups of students to the church is assuming that they can or even want to lead their peers to church. By the time popular teenagers realize they can lead or that they even want to lead, they have left your ministry and are off at college, and you have overlooked the potential of the other 90 percent of your ministry.

It's heartbreaking to observe this behavior, which was the very thing Jesus sought to change. Jesus would be furious if he stepped into some of our churches or para-church organizations and found that adults were picking and choosing only certain kids to spend time with. He would tell us what he told his disciples if we should prevent children from coming to Him: "If anyone causes one of these little ones—those who believe in me—to stumble, it would be better for them to have a large millstone hung around their neck and to be drowned in the depths of the sea." (Matthew 18:6).

Only picking a few of the little ones is preventing the rest from coming to him, and we ought to heed Jesus's warning. Jesus hung out with the outcasts, those on the fringe of society. He healed them, forgave them, and gave them purpose and value. Jesus noticed them when they were invisible to the culture around them. I've always navigated toward the different kids—the teenagers who others might overlook. I want them to know that I notice them, so they know that God sees them. Hannah taught me that.

One day, after our time in Colorado, I got a phone call from my mom saying they were thinking of moving back to our home state. It had only been a few years since Katie and I left Colorado, and it occurred to my mom that their reason for being in Colorado had ended. Hannah was an adult and didn't need protection from the horrors of her teenage years. My mom realized how much she enjoyed her grandkids and that her parents needed more and more assistance, so she started making plans to move, and my stepdad started looking for jobs.

Katie and I were shocked. What if we had stayed in Colorado? Would they have just left us there? Did God move us sooner so that we would all be together again? I'm not one to meddle with life scenarios that are in the past and completely out of our control, so I didn't dwell on that thought too much. I was more excited that after seven years of my parents and Hannah being in Colorado, they were finally ready to return home—or at least to the state where the majority of my mom's children and grandchildren were.

Christmas is my mom's favorite holiday and the one she would give up all the other holidays for. If she could ask for nothing else, it would be Christmas with all her children and grandchildren together. After college and before we were all married, it worked for several years for us older four children to travel to her, my stepdad, and Hannah in Colorado. I think my mom hoped that by moving back home, these festivities would continue, because the older four were married and two of us had kids, which made driving to Colorado not optimal.

I also recall my mom saying that Hannah was lonely the first Christmas that Katie and I missed, which was the Christmas after we left the Springs. I didn't realize at the time that Christmas was Hannah's favorite holiday too, and it was also when she was the most sensitive. Hannah wanted everything to go right and for everyone to get along because she knew it was important to my mom. She struggled with change and wasn't able to see that the dynamic of our childhood had changed.

Reliving the golden years once they are gone is impossible if not self-defeating. At some point in the seasons of life, it is good to recognize and acknowledge when something is good and enjoyable. However, when that season is over, sometimes you have to grieve the end of that season to prepare for the next. One of the stages of grief is denial, and I think both my mom and Hannah were in denial that our Christmases would be different, even when they eventually moved back home.

An acute medical issue struck my stepdad, and combined with his prospective job falling through, put a permanent move to Arizona in serious doubt. The next several months would be very fragile for us, because we were unsure of my stepdad's recovery time. My mom, stepdad, and Hannah needed to regroup and realize that it might not be the right time to move after all. Hannah called me and asked if she could come stay with us instead of in their rental home all alone.

"Of course," I said. "I know this is hard on you too."

She started crying, telling me how worried she was for her dad.

Hannah and her dad, my stepdad, had always been inseparable. It was my stepdad who would carry Hannah through the darkest times of despair and depression. When they moved to Colorado to give Hannah a fresh start, it became a testing ground for Hannah and her relationship with my mom and stepdad. She would continually test the boundaries, break curfew, get herself into all sorts of trouble, and continually admit that she needed help.

I recall a season of life when Hannah was working the night shift at the local grocery store. My stepdad would drive to the grocery store in the middle of the night and spend Hannah's dinner break with her. Every night Hannah worked, he showed up. He was a counselor by trade, and the best thing he knew he could do for Hannah was to be present. It seems that even the best therapists can still have trouble with their own children. All he could do was sit with Hannah and allow her to talk, and he would answer her questions when asked.

There was another time when Hannah moved out for a couple of months. My parents let her go, hoping it was a step of maturity. It turned out that the family Hannah lived with were drug users, and she got to a point where she was scared for her life. My stepdad immediately got in his SUV, drove to where Hannah was, packed up her stuff for her, and brought her home. It was like the story of the prodigal son, but instead of the son returning to the father, it was the father who went and fetched the son out of the pig filth he had landed in.

My stepdad invested everything he had into caring for his daughter. Through the ups and downs of Hannah's tumultuous teenage and early adult years, my stepdad was her constant. I think my stepdad having a sudden-onset acute condition shook her to her core. He was the strong one, and seeing her rock show signs of weakness worried Hannah.

Hannah made her way to our house to weather the storm of my mom and stepdad's absence. I knew this was an opportunity for me to show her love—to extend an olive branch for the years I had not been there for her. I knew Hannah had habits that annoyed me, like how she was a bit of a slob, but I also knew it wasn't an extended stay, so I was able to handle having her over without any conflict on my end. Hannah would tell me later how thankful she was for us that week. She was at the most fragile and worried place she had been in for years, and we provided the peace Hannah needed. After all, we lived with Hannah for months; now that we had a house of our own, we could extend the same help to her so she wouldn't be alone.

Being alone is one of the major anxieties and fears of someone with BPD. I didn't know it then, but I was giving Hannah exactly what she needed, which was not to be alone. I changed my expectations and knew Hannah would help herself to anything in our house. I knew she would sleep on the couch and make that her room. I knew Hannah probably wouldn't clean up after herself. She wasn't with us very long, and she had our little Levi to keep occupied, which helped Katie. I'm thankful that such a small gesture went so far with Hannah.

This armistice between us was successful because it was out of a moment of complete necessity that we came together so easily. We just had to wait to hear from mom about dad. Even though he wasn't my biological father, part of including Hannah into our giant mixed family was to consider her dad my dad too. I was so young when my mom remarried, I don't remember a time when I didn't have two dads. In conversations with Hannah, my mom, and stepdad, it was always just dad.

There were several unknown factors at this point for dad. We speculated that he could wait it out and easily find a job in Arizona, most likely in one of the metropolitan areas of connected cities in the state. It would place them farther away from us but still closer than Colorado. The other issue was that dad didn't snap back right away. He may have been cognizant and not paranoid, but he was still not himself. He would verbally tell me that he didn't think he was ever going to be the same again.

He was easy enough to be around. It didn't seem like there was a problem, but he just seemed to accept that this was his life now:

a broken person who couldn't work but fully trusted that whatever was going to happen was God's plan. The doctor had put him on medication and said it would take a few months for him to feel normal again. He left his job in Colorado after he'd used up his sick leave, and parted on good terms. The next issue was the house they planned to have built in Arizona. Once the construction company learned he had lost his job, he no longer qualified for the loan. That was enough to get them out of that big financial burden.

My mom, stepdad and Hannah eventually settled into a new home in a bigger city with a job that fit my stepdad's skill set. This new house on Jacob Avenue was their first home with a pool, and it became a getaway for my family. After our first Christmas with them, our desire to be closer to them grew. We eventually decided to leave my youth pastoring job and make a transition to be closer to them.

Our growing family was challenged so much the summer I left my final ministry job. Thankfully, my mom, stepdad, and Hannah were there to take care of my family while I finished working at the church. My sister swam every day with the boys. They went to the library, and Hannah and Kyle jumped back into the routine and friendship they'd had in Colorado. I found another reason for why we spent ten months in Colorado; God knew that Katie would need the relationship built with that part of my family for her to be comfortable living with them during that difficult transition for us. As much as I had been irritated in Colorado, God knew that Katie, Kyle, and now Levi would need the love of my mom, stepdad, and, most importantly, my sister Hannah, who had found her calling to be working with children.

Years after Hannah's passing, Katie, the kids, and I would decide to live with my mom and stepdad again. This part of the story I attribute to God's provision. It could only happen because of the nature of the relationship between my mom, my stepdad, and my wife. Our stay in the house on Jacob Avenue was the second time my family had converged on my mom and stepdad. This third time, we would share a home because my stepdad had decided it was time for him to retire. What tied us together now was our grief over losing Hannah.

I don't think I could have ever lived with Hannah again; that was clear in Colorado, and her short time staying with us was better but not permanent. I know it's no use speculating where my life would be if Hannah were still alive. Would she still be living with my parents? They admitted she might need their help her entire life several times. Would she be able to take care of herself after they died? Would one of us siblings need to look out for her or let her move in?

Before Hannah died, it was clear that her mental health and ability to be a fully functioning adult were debatable. Hannah would spend money that wasn't hers to spend. She couldn't hold a job past a year, if that. I don't think Hannah ever paid a bill in her life, not even for a car, phone, or credit card. Her BPD made the simplest tasks extremely difficult to teach, because Hannah would rather ask for forgiveness than ask for permission. Therefore, Hannah would inevitably be confronted on an issue and take it personally; rather than learn the actual lesson of responsibility, she would bear an emotional scar. Hannah couldn't remember to take her medications at the right time. My mom would take her to most of her doctor appointments. At twenty-four, it did not seem like Hannah was ready to be on her own.

My parents told me once back in Colorado that they were committed to love Hannah no matter what. If she needed to live with them and have them care for her, they would. They would still hold to boundaries with Hannah, so she wouldn't be able to do whatever she wanted. Hannah was very much under their authority in terms of following their rules. The rules were basic rules: come home quietly, don't leave a mess in the kitchen, do your own laundry, and don't leave dishes in your room.

They did not treat Hannah like a teenager, as some parents do when their children don't leave home. They let Hannah be an adult, but they were trying to teach her how to be a good roommate, because their goal was for her to someday find someone she could marry, and if not, then at least find a healthy roommate to live with. The best way they could help her was to train her to be a healthy person to live with and come alongside her in love through her failures and shortcomings.

This was something I failed to see in my heart. My sibling jealousy blinded me to this level of compassion from parents to their child. I was the prodigal son's brother, or really the prodigal daughter's brother, the one jealous for my parents' attention.

My mom and stepdad and my wife and I sold our two houses and moved into one large house. It was a mansion fit for a king—or family of eight, something beyond a blessing. My mom and stepdad still live with me; we have an attached apartment that suits their needs. When my mom wants to host parties, we have a giant open living room to fit all the grandchildren. Hannah would approve and be happy to know that her mom and dad are well cared for in her absence.

The pain I carried from Colorado continued to subside as God revealed the pieces he was moving into position. When I saw failure and somehow missing a sign from God, he reminded me that there is no plan B. He showed me, after the fact, how His plan was taking the worst circumstances and creating a life that embraces a God who is always at work. Leaving my job led me to my here and now, and my here and now I would not change.

Looking back, I wonder if I lost touch with the way Hannah was speaking. I assumed wrong intent based on my understanding of words and what she intended by them. In any relationship, especially a marriage relationship, understanding not just what is said but the intent behind it could be the most important aspect of a relationship. The best relationship advice I was given was to say, "This is what I heard. Is this what you meant?" It allows others to hear their own words back to themselves, like a mirror for our vocal cords. The other person can either say, "Yes" or "No, that was not the intent behind what I said."

You can never assume someone else's intent until you ask. That is the key to what happened when I stopped communicating with Hannah. I never tried to understand her intent. I just looked at the action, made a judgment, and never gave her the benefit of the doubt. The Colorado confrontation arose from me not simply asking her, "Hannah, I heard you say or do this. Is this what you meant?" I think that would have helped a lot. I have so many things I regret not saying or doing differently with her.

If you are like me, you become part of your parent's retirement, and you buy a house together so they can have their private retirement community with an attached common area large enough to host family get-togethers. My parent's investment in me, I suppose, is going on thirty-four-plus years now. I at least pay my half of the mortgage and utilities. The only time I didn't pay for rent was as a poor grad student with a wife, a child, and no job, and that was when I was twenty-five. Nowadays, our family model is called a multigenerational home.

When you have grandparents around, you have to accept their advice and recognize they don't follow it because they are not parents anymore. It's not their job to raise my children; it's my job. It would be foolish of me to ignore their advice when they have over thirty-six years of parenting expertise. It is hard to admit you don't have it all figured out with your children. I think there are some proverbs in there somewhere, seeking wise counsel (Proverbs 15:22 and 19:20) or pursuing wisdom and the like; Proverbs 4 is a good place to start. My parents are that for me, and they have humbled me.

Honestly, if Hannah were still alive, I don't think I would be hearing what they are telling me now. If Hannah were still here, we wouldn't be living in this multigenerational home. The Colorado experiment didn't work, and it wouldn't be until years after her death that I would realize that Colorado was where my wife got to know my mom and stepdad and build a relationship with them. Our current living situation only works because of that time in Colorado on Stone Fence Drive. I don't regret Colorado today, as I did back then. Today it is clear: Colorado wasn't just for me to go to school, it was for me, Katie, Kyle, my mom, and my stepdad to learn to become a family.

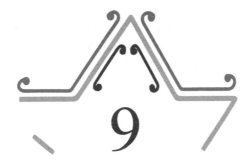

9

Wandering in the Desert

When we moved into the house on Jacob Avenue in Arizona, it was Stone Fence Drive all over again, but this time my sister was right down the hallway. I knew in the back of my mind that I needed to not be combative or confrontational with her this time around, since it didn't work last time. Instead, I went to the other extreme of spending the least amount of time with her as possible. What that translated into was me ignoring her.

I don't think I blatantly ignored her as a form of malice. I was doing my best not to respond negatively, but I just ended up not responding at all. On top of me trying to walk on eggshells around her, I had the added pressure of needing to find a job. Once it was clear that I would be leaving my previous job, and it was also clear that I was not going to receive any of the three jobs I was aiming for, I changed career paths. I realized that maybe it was time to do the thing I had put off for eight years, which was teaching.

The summer is not the best time to start looking for teaching positions. Schools make hiring decisions during contract renewals in the middle of the spring semester. I would be looking for bottom-of-the-barrel teaching positions that I qualified for with no experience.

We lived with my mom, stepdad, and Hannah for a few weeks. Well, *I* was only in their house for three weeks; Katie and the kids were there three times longer. I knew very clearly from previous experience that I could not stay with my sister. The reality was that living with Hannah was next to impossible. My mom would even tell me as a form of validating my feelings, "She can be a difficult person to love. However, we still are required to love her." That didn't help. How do you love a difficult person who intentionally makes it hard for you to show love toward her unless you give in to everything she wants?

If Hannah had an opinion on something, it wasn't enough to listen; you had to agree or take her advice. If you didn't take her advice or you disagreed with her opinion, Hannah would be offended. It was a lose-lose conversation. Katie was much better at befriending Hannah than I was, from back in the house on Stone Fence Drive to the Jacob Avenue house. Katie was great at being agreeable and letting a lot of things slide that I would want to go to battle over. Katie kept the molehills molehills, while I would get lost in the rocky terrain of the Sierra Nevadas. A lot of how Katie functioned for Hannah was as a listening board, but they also still had books in common. I think that was helpful for both of them. You can talk to a person for a long time about one book, and they would read upwards of thirty books a year.

On top of that, I think being the same gender helped. Katie and Hannah enjoyed doing crafts—not that boys can't, but shopping for crafts is just as bad and agonizing for me as shopping for clothes. Hannah also helped Katie with the kids, tremendously. While I failed to recognize her help with Kyle when we lived in Colorado, it became very clear to me how much she helped with Levi in the months Katie was living in the Jacob Avenue house as I finished up my ministry position, and the months after, when we had found an apartment a few cities over in the same metropolitan area. I think, too, that Katie needed a friend—someone to talk to and relate to, and someone who loved her kids as much as she did. Katie's view of Hannah was that of a sister-in-law. She took that role seriously and knew that ultimately, no matter how difficult Hannah was, Hannah was a blessing.

When I decided to switch from ministry to teaching, the only reason I had any motivation to study was thanks to Hannah, who quizzed me nonstop for a week straight. I made flash cards. We would all be swimming, and Hannah would read my flash cards to me and make sure I had committed the information to memory. That was a moment where we saw each other as equals. Hannah was trying to achieve the same goal of becoming an elementary teacher, and would eventually need to take the same test. It was a level playing field for us. I needed help studying, and Hannah was more than happy to learn the material herself. I passed that first test with flying colors thanks to Hannah.

I think God humbled me, lowered my position and status, took away my salary, and forced me to be at the same level as Hannah. His process of refining me before her death softened my heart to take the blow. I am not sure if I would have responded to her death the same if my heart was still as hardened as it was when we left Colorado. So many times, Hannah could have lost her life, but God was preparing me for the trial to come. What I thought was the trial—losing a job and moving—was the preparation before the true test of my faith.

It perplexes me to this day. Why did Hannah think it was okay to take images off my phone without asking? I realize my response could have waited or been better delivered. I know it was an appropriate boundary for me to have, but I was so caught off guard by Hannah's lack of respect for our privacy. She also wasn't even trying to cover her tracks by deleting the text messages she sent herself, so I know there was some break in perspective on her part. Maybe it has something to do with Hannah's BPD and inability to truly see something from someone else's perspective. I thought I handled it appropriately, but I left the situation with the same feeling that I usually get whenever I say something wrong to Hannah.

Hannah was happy to stay with the boys while I was at the hospital. I had expected her to be asleep, but she was awake when I dashed home to change out clothes and supplies. Everything was great between us. The new baby had arrived, and it was a girl. Hannah couldn't be more thrilled. She hugged me and said she was so excited, and then she asked if I had pictures. I gave her my phone and told her she could look at them while I ran upstairs and threw on shorts, a shirt, and sandals. I got my toiletry needs and grabbed what Katie requested.

I returned back downstairs with a small bag in hand, Hannah gave me my phone back and thanked me for letting her look at the pictures. I hugged her and thanked her for helping us with the boys. I told her she could come hopefully the following day and see the new little one as soon as the NICU said it was okay for visitors.

At some point the next day, I was on my phone and noticed that Hannah had posted to Facebook and tagged Katie and me. I clicked on the notification, and to my utter shock, surprise, dismay, and frustration there were photos from my phone on her post. This wasn't the first time Hannah had posted something of ours that was private, so it wasn't a rookie error. There had been several conversations over the past years about invading someone else's space and not doing it on social media as well. That was one piece of the problem. The even bigger one for me was that Hannah had taken pictures off of my phone.

I looked at my texts, and sure enough, Hannah had sent herself virtually every single photo taken that night—before, during, and after Emallyn's birth. Hannah had helped herself to all of them, and I was fuming. My blood was boiling. It was Colorado all over again. Hannah had not changed one bit, and clearly my response to her had not changed.

I showed Katie, and she was upset too. That gave me even more justification for my out-of-control feelings. I was already sleep-deprived, emotionally exhausted, and not at my best—and then I found this major invasion of our privacy. Hannah never asked to have a copy of what I considered very private photos. These photos were only meant for me and Katie to share, and maybe one day Emi if she wanted to see. I thought I was being nice and loving by even letting Hannah see the photos that night when she asked. I was letting her into my very personal life.

As a guy—and many guys would attest to this—the need for privacy is monumental. Airing your dirty laundry on social media usually comes across as a sign of weakness. I'm not saying this is correct, but there is a reality in life among adult males that plays out very clearly in children and most abundantly in middle school when they hit adolescence. All this to say, my adolescent instincts kicked in after the boundary of personal space was demolished by Hannah taking photos from my phone without asking.

Hannah didn't stop there. She then proceeded to make our baby announcement for us. I think we had posted something initially that formalized at least the fact that our baby Emallyn, or Emi, was born and needed prayers. Hannah took that as liberty to make a giant post and attach maybe eight to ten pictures taken from my phone. To her credit, Hannah was selective with the pictures and chose appropriate ones and not any that would be embarrassing to Katie. However, to take photos without asking and then break our Facebook rule of posting without permission was too much.

I knew that if I talked to Hannah, it would not go well. I had been doing my best to not "poke the bear," as they say about short-fused creatures. For Hannah, it wasn't a fuse of anger or rage but a fuse of a complete emotional breakdown. I decided I just needed to focus on the Facebook post and kindly ask her to take it down. I would allow her to keep the photos if she could keep them private. Fighting her on taking the photos was not necessary when the real problem was her sharing something that wasn't hers to share. I made a decision from that point on that if Hannah asked to see pictures, I would either say no or just show them to her myself. I would never hand my phone to her again. I drew an internal line that placed my heart at yet another great distance from Hannah. I chose not to trust her because I couldn't confront her without causing more damage than I had in past confrontations.

When Hannah came to pick up my mom and take her home after seeing Emi, I also got to see the boys, hug them and reassure them mommy was okay, and their baby sister was okay. I asked Hannah in the best voice I could, not raising my tone or attacking, "Hey, Hannah, we are not ready to have people post things on Facebook about Emi. Could you take that down?"

She stared at me, trying to read my emotions and intent, and just said, "Okay."

I found out later Hannah just cried on the way home. She didn't cry in front of me because I had become unsafe for her to cry in front of, but my mom would do her best to try to figure out what happened. Mom seemed like the best one to reason with Hannah.

For Hannah, this was more than just the Facebook post. It was the fact that I was confronting her again. Anytime someone confronts a person with BPD, the person relives every past conflict as well and sees them all as one built on top of the other. When people with BPD are confronted, you are literally opening a can of worms of all past conflicts. Hannah sees the current conflict with all the other conflicts and emotions behind them running at her at full tilt. Hannah's reaction was what I saw as self-pity.

My mom told me Hannah spent the time on their drive home crying that we would never have the relationship she wanted, that she messed up again, and that I was mad at her. I knew this was going to happen; Hannah had become very predictable. I weighed my options and decided that making a request to remove the Facebook post was the safest because avoiding it wasn't an option. Also, if I either untagged myself or unfriended her, Hannah would have received that passive aggressive maneuver as much worse.

Hannah obliged and deleted the post. This was the last disagreement before the Halloween debacle the following month, when I realized I should not discuss plans at all with her and instead just speak my mind honestly to my mom as she fielded the balls of emotions and questions between Hannah and me. The invasion of privacy of the photos taken from my phone led me to be unable to talk to her directly about our Halloween plans at our apartment. It was all I was left with as a method of keeping our relationship.

I didn't want Hannah to run my life, but I also didn't want to continue to be a problem for her. Neither confronting nor apathy were working. When my mom presented me with the Halloween "molehill" request, which I in turn made into a mountain, I was actually able to process ahead of time what really mattered so that I could accommodate Hannah in some fashion. Instead of a no to everything, or a yes, I offered a compromise that my mom was able to get Hannah to agreeably accept, even though I was bothered by the request.

Hannah and I reconciled the conversation about the photos on one of our walks taking Katie to the NICU. Only one extra family member was allowed in at a time, so Hannah and I let my mom have a turn. Hannah brought up the photos and apologized. This was a completely different Hannah than the one in Colorado. She cried and said she didn't want to mess up our relationship, and I apologized back. I apologized for being difficult and for not saying things in a kinder, more gentle way. I said I forgave her and asked if she would forgive me for my brashness. We had a good conversation and hugged.

It was really a reconciliation of our summer as well, where we both recognized that our relationship was not where we wanted it to be. It was a start. If we'd had more time, we would have probably had to go to counseling to figure out exactly how we needed to communicate. Hannah had a therapist she saw weekly, and I would learn later that the therapist provided much insight for my mom about Hannah. The counselor would later provide insight into my relationship with Hannah as well.

The counselor provided insight into how Hannah viewed me before she passed away. The counselor shared how Hannah had viewed me her entire life and helped explain some of Hannah's actions and reactions to me. The time I spent meeting with the counselor after Hannah's death helped me shift my regret and move toward a place of acceptance. I would find comfort and peace with Hannah through her counselor's words. My last day of regret would finally be understood after that visit.

Without faith, you cannot see God. God cannot perform His wonders if you do not even believe he exists (Hebrews 11:6). Everything will be seen through your human eyes until you put on the mind of Christ and realize God has been working the whole time.

It is still taking time for my mom to come to accept the road God started them on once they left Colorado. They went to Colorado for Hannah, and their return from Colorado would ultimately be for Hannah. She would take her last breath under the same rising and setting sun she was born under. Her death would be both the end that God brought my mom and stepdad to and the end he brought me to. Why did he bring us to that end, at that time and in that place?

The Spirit, in these darkest moments in our life, is still good and has not abandoned us. "Be strong and courageous. Do not be afraid or terrified because of them, for the Lord your God goes with you; he will never leave you nor forsake you" (Deuteronomy 31:6). Would you rather be in despair, blame and reject God, and have it all be without purpose? Or be in despair and have hope? We choose to be in despair, recognize the darkness, and hold firmly to what faith we have and can gather in such a time of great loss. Jesus promised that even faith the size of a small seed as the mustard seed can grow into something bigger than ourselves (Luke 17:6). He never promised the amount of time it would take to grow, but he did say it would grow.

God tested our faith. My mom and stepdad took a slow and steady pace, but I was catapulted forward at an incalculable rate of change. The divergence of our two paths, in time, began to represent the spectrum of grief, guilt, regret, and healing people take. The cause of pain is the same, but the severity of the wound has to do with the proximity to the pain, the relationship with the pain, and the leading of the Spirit.

I look back even now and see the Spirit leading us, but at different times and to different places. Same God, same good God that is not a one size or type God. He is not a God who is fashioned by man's understanding that one must conform to. God will reveal Himself to His people the way His people need to see Him or are best able to recognize Him. Looking back on everything that happened in the rental house and my mom, stepdad, and Hannah's eventual move to the new house on Jacob Avenue, I found God's providence in the end.

10

A Series of Unpredictable Events

Amazingly, Emi ended up only needing two weeks in the hospital, not four, as had been originally predicted. Her lungs were healthy, and she was gaining weight. The second week was the hardest for Katie, because they discharged her from the hospital but not Emi. That meant we had to go home without our baby. No one expects to deliver a baby and then go home without one. It was painful; it was as if somehow there was no baby or we had lost the baby. To not be able to be home with our newborn was heartbreaking.

Katie spent every day of the next week at the hospital for as long as she could. I went back to work and took care of Kyle. My mom and Hannah would help with Levi the whole week. I don't remember that week much. I just remember when they finally said our baby could come home. That was when the real work began.

It was in the middle of this sleep deprivation regimen of dealing with a colicky baby while trying not to forget the other two children, and living in a tiny apartment that the first day of regret would force its way to the forefront of my life. I would drop everything to face head-on the despair, and shock that was waiting for me at the house on Jacob Avenue.

I cannot even begin to describe the message on my cell phone and the phone conversation I had with my mother that Friday morning. I thought it strange that my mom would call me when I was at work, and I had a hunch that maybe I should check the message. Her voice showed the same fear and panic it did when my stepdad went through his nervous break. I stood in the hallway right outside my classroom and pressed *play* on my phone's voice message app. I had only heard my mom say my name that way when my stepdad had his sudden-onset medical crises, but this time it was worse than I had imagined it could be said.

In a split second, even before my mother began her cries for help and begged me to come to her quickly, I knew that something was wrong. On the message, she said my name in a high-pitched, desperate cry and then for a moment let out a mourning wail. "Come quick, Matt Jo," she said with another wail. "Her lips are blue. Come quick." She then let out a cry of deep despair and fear before hanging up the phone. Mom was referring to my sister Hannah.

I held on to this message for a few years; I listened to it a few times during moments of emptiness, hoping to feel some sort of sadness or emotion from this painful memory that had numbed me. Moments of emptiness that are worse than the moments of tears. With tears come feelings—and having feelings, even sad ones, is better than feeling numb. Feeling numb is not living; it is simply not dying. I would rather cry over the death of my sister than feel numb or apathetic. I feel like it is a disservice to Hannah's life to feel nothing at all, as if she has left no mark on my life.

Hannah of all people understood what it meant to feel something in everything, sometimes to her disadvantage. I want to always feel something when I think of her. I held onto this message for as long as I could. I have only shared it with my wife, since it felt kind of morbid, but I never wanted to lose the feeling I experienced that moment, one of both fear and purpose. I needed to get to my mom. She needed me.

My deepest fear for Hannah was that she had committed suicide. I immediately told the teacher next to me that I had to make an emergency phone call and could he please watch my class. I walked out onto the grass and called my mother, hoping she would pick up. The same muffled, high-pitched sobs came from the other end of the phone. All my mom could muster was the phrase that Hannah's lips were blue.

I told her she needed to call 911. "You always call 911 first, Mom!" I had wrongly assumed that I was her first phone call; the last time there was a phone call like this, I was the first person she called.

Mom finally was able to say, "They are here," referring to the paramedics working to resuscitate Hannah. My mom could only repeat back to me, "Her lips are blue. They are working on her."

Hannah had picked this house out when they had moved back from Colorado the previous year. She told my mom and stepdad that she wanted a pool for herself and her nieces and nephews. After weeks of looking, this was the house that the three of them had agreed upon. I remember Hannah saying the realtor was mean to her; Hannah was giving her opinion, and the realtor stopped talking to her and just talked to my parents. The realtor did not understand that my parents had already made the life choice to allow Hannah to live with them for as long as it took for her to be on her own. They had made a choice to love her above all else, and that meant a different set of expectations than they had for the older four of us kids.

I was always mad at Hannah—jealous and frustrated that she was taking all my parents time and energy. She was twenty-four years old. Why couldn't she have gone off to college like the rest of us, gotten a job, and been on her own? I recall thinking to myself when Hannah was complaining about the realtor, *Even the realtor assumes you should be on your own and not giving your opinion on the house that our mom and dad buy.*

It wasn't until that unexpected Friday phone call from my mom that I understood why they had made the choice to love her and help her regardless. What I understood was that they knew the preciousness of life. They didn't know how long they would have Hannah if they did not choose to love her unconditionally. It was as if God, in a miraculous intervention of knowing the length of Hannah's life, told my parents that loving her was the best gift they could ever give her and themselves.

With the grim hope of Hannah's current condition, my parents had placed a bet on Hannah's emotional wellbeing years ago, and it would pay out tenfold that Friday when Hannah died. Had they chosen the route of severing a relationship with her because she was not adhering to their expectations, they would have lost precious time with her. Instead, they mended the relationship at every corner, picking Hannah back up and forgiving her at every hurdle and mistake. This effort afforded them the time that they didn't know was limited to spend together. Several years with Hannah were savored, from her eighteenth year of life until her death.

When Hannah was supposed to be on her own, my parents invested all their time into her limited amount of time. The years of allowing Hannah to live with them and be nurtured into adulthood would be worth it. My parents had made the right choice to love her unconditionally all those years ago.

Once I understood that Mom had already called for help and that the paramedics were working on Hannah, although I was not clear about her condition and perhaps did not want to know in that moment, I said to my mom that I was on my way. She said, "Okay," and that was it. I hung up the phone and ran to find my principal. He happened to be in the next hallway over. I stopped him and said I had to go—I had a family emergency. No questions asked, he just looked at me, saw the fear in my face, and said, "Go, get out of here. I'll take care of your class."

I shut down my laptop, packed everything up in a minute, didn't even look at my class, and said on my way out the door that I had a family emergency to take care of. I asked the teacher next door to please watch my class until the principal showed up. He agreed as I proceeded down the hallway.

I reached Kyle's second-grade class a minute later and found him at his desk. I told his teacher we needed to leave for a family emergency, and she too saw the fear in my face and said, "Of course, go." My son was trying to put his binder in his backpack, and his teacher told him not to worry about it—to just take his backpack and go.

On our way to the car, my son asked why we were leaving early, and I didn't really know what to share with him. I knew that he understood death—his grandpa had passed away two years prior—but I couldn't tell him and remain strong. In that moment in the parking lot, trying to hold back tears, I decided that it wasn't best for him to know what was happening. I was in a state of panic myself, and it would not help my son to see his father panicked. Not that I shouldn't be honest with him or show emotion with him; I just realized that as a parent, sometimes we have to carry burdens for our children. The burden of his aunt dying was not something I could carry with him at that moment, and I instead decided just to hold it for him and allow him to enjoy the life of a seven-year-old. Growing up would come soon enough for him; I just wanted him to remain a kid for another day. Tomorrow would be a better day for me to be able to carry this burden with him.

As we walked, I told him that Jomama, the name he used for my mom, needed my help. When Kyle first met my mom, I was still Joey to him. Before Katie and I were married, Katie introduced my mom to him and said, "This is Joey's mom." Kyle heard some version of "Joey" and "mama," and the name Jomama came out of his mouth. To this day, we still call her Jomama.

As we drove, I had to decide if I should tell my wife about the phone call. Again, the protective instinct kicked in, and I realized that I couldn't carry the burden with her either. I would have to call her and tell her there was something wrong with her sister in-law, her friend.

I think Katie, being an outsider to our family drama, had fresh eyes with Hannah. It allowed her to love Hannah unconditionally. It is more likely that it is simply in Katie's nature to love people no matter who they were. She loved Hannah, and I couldn't tell her what had happened over a phone call, with her being all alone in our small apartment, with a two-month-old baby and our two-year-old son.

When we left Colorado in a hurry, I was eager to be out on my own with my wife and son and didn't really take the time to say my last goodbyes to Hannah. I had crushed her spirit, invalidated her feelings, and bullied her into submission. Looking back, I could have waited a whole month before I moved, but I wanted to punish Hannah for how she treated me. I could have given her more time to process us leaving, but instead, out of anger, I moved sooner than planned. I rationalized to myself, *Hannah, you did this to yourself. If you were not so difficult to love and stayed out of my personal life, I would have stayed a few more weeks.* I was happy to leave; my wife, son and I needed our own space and to be a family.

The fact that I left wasn't the problem; it was how I left that caused the most pain. Out of all the things I regret with Hannah, leaving Colorado as quickly as I did, without spending quality time with her and giving her a chance to soak up more time with my son and wife and even me, is at the top of my list. Of course, when faced with death, we all regret. We all wish we had more time with a loved one. We all wish we could take back things we said or did. We punish ourselves in our grief with our regrets. If the first stage of grief is shock, then the second is regret.

My family moving away from Colorado reminds me of the verse, "In your anger do not sin" (Ephesians 4:26). I was angry, and I allowed it to cloud my judgment in how I treated Hannah. Hearing from my stepdad, after her passing, that Hannah was heartbroken when we left brought tears to my eyes. I had intentionally caused my sister pain, and I never got to openly admit why I left as quickly as I did. I never told my parents the real reason for leaving. It was all under the guise of needing to start my new job, but I never told them that I had a month to get there.

My stepdad was right: guys tend to withhold emotion as a form of punishment to the people closest to them. I regret that I withheld forgiveness from Hannah, and I regret most of all that I withheld a relationship with her older brother from her. I withheld the brother who rushed to the hospital when she was fourteen because she was suicidal and prayed over her. I withheld the brother who would take Hannah and her friends to late-night concerts when she was in high school. I withheld the brother who brought roses to Hannah's school on her sixteenth birthday. I withheld my compassion for her.

The day Hannah died, I found that compassion. It was buried beneath layers of defensiveness, comparison, anger, bitterness, jealousy, impossible expectations, judgment, and fear. The day Hannah died, all those things disappeared. There was no one to hold a grudge against except myself, and that seemed senseless to me at the time.

When I was faced with the death of my sister, all my negative feelings became meaningless, pointless, weightless, and no longer valid. I could finally see myself and Hannah without all the pain in between. What I saw in me was a broken heart, and would lead me toward repentance that day and in the days to come.

I called my sister-in-law, Mandi, who lived on the way from my work to my mom's house. I said I had an emergency and needed her to take Kyle home to Katie for me. I said I would explain everything when we met. I ended up meeting Mandi in a Walmart parking lot, where Kyle agreeably got into his aunt's car.

I looked at my sister-in-law and said, "I think my sister committed suicide, and I have to go help my mom."

She burst into tears and hugged me, saying, "I'm so sorry."

I had never seen Mandi cry. She was the strong-willed one, between her and Katie. Seeing her break down instantly broke down my emotional barrier I had constructed for Kyle's sake. We hugged and cried, and I asked her if she could tell my wife in person. I didn't want Katie to be alone at home with two small children and not have anyone to comfort her.

My sister-in-law nodded in agreement and said, "Of course!"

I got in the car and begin to weep again, even more than I had with my sister-in-law. This was the same mournful wail I'd heard coming from my mother. Fear was what broke through first. Anyone can die at any time, for any reason, and we have absolutely no control over it. At the same time, I was prepared, and as the day unfolded, I was ready to respond. Many people are held down and left immobile when a crisis strikes, but my thoughts prepared me to take action that day. I became a man on a mission, one who would be able to respond to the emergency and devastation that had hit my family.

11

The First Day of Regret

Death is not someone you want to befriend. You do not keep company with death, nor do you wish to associate with him. My mother, weeks later, would describe being the parent of a child who died as like being in an exclusive club—only no one chose to be a member. As I walked through the ER doors and proceeded down the hallway to the room I'd been directed to, the silence from the nurses confirmed that death was waiting at the end of this path. My legs could not carry me any faster, yet I wished I would not get to where I was going at all, to avoid the inevitable.

The hairs on my arms made themselves known to me as I stepped through the sliding glass door. I knew what I was about to see, and I made a conscious choice at that moment to accept what had happened and be strong. Not that I wasn't going to be sad or devastated, but I was going to be in control of my reality. I was not going to allow my mind to give in to confusion or obsessiveness. I would tackle this horror head-on.

My sister was dead, and there was a long dark pathway we needed to traverse. My family would need someone with a lamp to show them the way. This light would be hope, and I had more of it than I gave myself credit for. My hope centered on the revelation that I knew *why* I was *where* I was. I knew why I was doing what I was doing and going through these difficult circumstances. In the two hours between leaving school and walking into that room, I found my purpose. My life and Hannah's life became inextricably linked, and I could not deny the fact that I had arrived in this life circumstance, for the exact purpose of experiencing this moment.

There wasn't just a long road ahead; I had already been traveling down a painful path. I had lost my way for months, wandering in the desert, and Hannah's death gave me direction. My family would join me on the unknown journey that death had set us on, but I had already been wandering aimlessly. If you observe the lay of the land of a new place for any amount of time, you become accustomed to the terrain. I was aware that I had been traveling in circles and this tragedy brought direction, meaning, and purpose to my pain. These things would become more apparent within the coming weeks.

My mother, still the caring and nurturing person she'd always been, asked each of us who came into the room if we wanted to see Hannah one more time. Even when faced with death, she expressed concern for the rest of us, wanting to protect us from this pain. Without hesitation, I said yes. I don't know what I was expecting to see, but there she was: my Hannah just as I remembered her, and at the same time undeniably gone.

You might think seeing a dead body would be a horrible experience. But somehow, we still saw life within her lifeless body. It was probably the utter shock and adrenaline that allowed us to process being in the same room with Hannah. Her body was stiff. An endotracheal tube protruded from her mouth, and pink foamy vomit surrounded it. She was blue-faced, with eyes closed, head propped back, and chin up. Hannah's tattoos of the Ethiopian cross with two birds on each side were visible higher up on her chest, and the writing on her wrist was visible as well.

She had gotten the giant cross when she returned from a mission trip to Ethiopia, along with the writing on her wrist. It looked like

Arabic symbols but was in fact Amharik, the native language of Ethiopia. The symbols translate to, "I am healed."

I remember that trip being difficult for her. She didn't feel included in the team. The college ministry she was part of in Colorado was great, but for some reason, Hannah didn't feel welcomed on the smaller team that went to Ethiopia to work with children. I also think it's just hard to go to new places and see poverty in the poorest parts of the world.

Ethiopia challenged her but also grew her deeply. Seeing other people hurting is a surefire way to pull yourself out of your own problems and see that you are not the only one. God took her across the world, and her tattoos showed that she'd allowed God to begin His heart work within her.

The cross and the word—pronounced *danku*—written in Amharik on her wrist said a lot about Hannah's reflections on that trip. However, part of the difficulty for her involved her BPD. Hannah read into actions immensely, so molehills to her felt like mountains, thus any conflict was interpreted as a personal attack. I also think Hannah had an extraordinary amount of empathy for other people, and what appeared to be self-focused feelings were really her connecting to other broken people on a deeper level.

Hannah knew brokenness personally, and she was empathetic toward every hurting person she came into contact with. Even though Hannah could read people—see their heart and true intentions—her response to this level of discernment was the problem. It is as if the amplification of other people's emotions put her in a defensive position. What people perceived as Hannah being emotional was actually her response to this amplification of other people's emotions behind their words. It isn't just what we say, it's how we say things and the body language when we speak. All these components, for Hannah, was like walking into a building with the fire alarm going off.

Maybe one of the reasons why I shut her out is because I did not want her to see my mistakes, either as a new husband or as a new dad. I was too insecure and immature to admit to the imperfections that she might see in me. When I reacted to her out of my own defensiveness, the emotion she felt from her brother was like a clanging symbol.

The blue in Hannah's face was the most abnormal part of the scene in that ER room. My mind could trick itself into believing that the tube was allowing her to breath; after all, tubes in mouths are in every medical television show. Her laying so still on the hospital bed could be easily construed as a simple coma. What my brain could not comprehend was the coldness. The blue in the pigment of her skin was like ice. It was if she died of hypothermia. Hannah's forehead was cold to the touch, as if she had just come in from playing out in the snow, like when we were children.

My parents told me that by law, they could not remove anything placed on Hannah's body during the process of trying to revive her. This is not the normal procedure, but because of Hannah's age and the suddenness of her death, the county required an autopsy. My parents had no say in the matter; Hannah's body would be taken away and given to the county medical examiner's office. We were told initially it could take weeks and to plan accordingly, as if the coroner would not have her body released to us. These realities were not on my parents' minds, but they were fresh on my mind the minute I walked into the room. I knew from my ministry experience that we would need a service within the week, and we would need to make additional arrangements for when we actually received Hannah's body.

As my mind raced through these details, my parents further informed me that the medical examiner's office would not be able to retrieve my sister's body for five or six hours and therefore, to take all the time I needed with Hannah, since we did not know when we would see her again. It's ironic that we thought in terms of when our next opportunity would be to see Hannah, when all along she was dead and we would never get to see her alive again. We wanted to soak in every moment with her that we could, dead or alive. Personally, I wanted to see Hannah for as long as possible before she was embalmed. Even though she was younger than the other family members I'd seen in their caskets, I knew that she would not look like she did in that hospital emergency room, once embalmed.

Blood was dripping out of Hannah's nose every few minutes, and my stepdad, mother, and I took turns wiping it away to keep her face clean. My stepdad had started cleaning the blood with a Kleenex minutes after they pronounced her dead. I soon asked for a rag, and the nurse brought a stack. Minute by minute, as Hannah's blood drained from her nostrils, we cleaned it, wiping away what vitality was left in her.

At one point, I had wiped the blood up toward her eye, and it appeared as if there was a trail of red tears. We opened her eyelids, and there she was. Her pupils were not dilated, and it looked like she was staring back up at us. We knew Hannah was dead, but at moments, she seemed very much alive. We rubbed her face and hands for hours.

Later, after my older twin sisters traveled two and a half hours to the hospital, they lay across her body sobbing uncontrollably for what seemed like forever. My stepdad could not hold back the complete emptiness from his face. He would stand by Hannah, and then sit down on the other side of her in a chair with his head in his hands. He would go back to Hannah and whisper to himself, "Just take a breath, baby, just take another breath." He was pleading for his baby girl to come back to him. My mother kept recycling two or three statements as if convincing herself of a truth that was hard to swallow.

After a couple of hours, I stepped out into the hallway to call Katie. We had been texting back and forth since she'd found out what had happened from her sister Mandi. She would tell me later that she didn't believe what had happened until I called and told her Hannah was gone. The reality sunk in for her then, and her tears came.

For Katie, her sister-in-law—and at times her only friend—had died. For Mandi, seeing Katie broken and her brother-in-law in such distress broke her as well. Mandi, was caught up in the emergency of the day, and rightly so. Only a heartless person would ignore the palpable grief in the air.

Mandi had a large amount of empathy, and she stuck to the task I had given her, which I found most valuable at a time when I could not be there myself. She gave Katie her support when mine was absent. In the wake of death, the presence of others is most needed. The void from a missing life has to be filled not with words but with the presence of the living. Death brings great loneliness and despair. People who have lost someone to death need the presence of other souls from the land of the living.

I was in shock and disbelief, even as I stood before Hannah's lifeless body on the table in the ER. I still couldn't wrap my mind around her being dead. I asked Katie if she wanted to come to see Hannah before the coroner's office came to retrieve her body; but Katie declined, saying she didn't want to see Hannah as I had described her.

Hannah's age and the suddenness of her death automatically opened an investigation by the local police. Hannah was too young to die of natural causes, so the police needed to do their due diligence to decide what kind of death this was: suicide, homicide, accident, or a medical condition. My poor mom would have to go into every single detail with the police of what happened that morning when she arrived home from her morning workout. This was her burden to carry for my stepdad. She was positive it would have been too much for him to bear if he was the one to find her lifeless body on the couch that morning and then relive it for the police.

As much pain as my mom was in, she said that her message from God was that it had to be her. More than that, she was the only one who could have carried this unimaginable burden. My mom's faith was always the strongest of us all, and this would stretch her faith beyond what was humanly possible. My mom had learned, before I was even born, that when pain strikes, we must lean into God, and lean she did.

My mom could grieve immensely and cry out to God not in anger but with unrelenting submission and faith. As long as I can remember, she never hid her feelings from God; she always allowed God's presence in every burden and joy. My mom had been preparing her entire life to take on this tragic and horrific event: the death of her daughter and the death of her husband's only child. I don't think either one of them could have gone through this alone, but my mom's part in getting Hannah to the hospital was something she was well equipped to do.

Through every tear, she compressed Hannah's chest with all her might. She prayed for life to come back to Hannah's lips. My mom recalled that Hannah was to heavy too move her of the couch, so she called an ambulance, and immediately began CPR until the paramedics arrived. She just kept saying, "No, Hannah, No!"

When the paramedics got there and relieved her of the burden of performing chest compressions and counting, she stood back and began to lose herself. She made two phone calls: one to my stepdad and the second to me. I pray she will never have to call me again with the message of "Come quick, I need you." Her words, voice, tears, pain, desperation, and mournful wail are forever seared into the crevices of my mind.

It had been several hours, and the emergency was beginning to subside as the reality of what we were facing sunk in, at least for me. My stepdad says he doesn't remember much from that day or the following months. His brain's way of coping with what happened was to go into hibernation. When our pain is too great, our mind stops holding the memories of those moments, or it locks them away into its furthest recesses and barricades it from any feeling.

My stepdad says he doesn't remember me in the ER that day; he doesn't remember Thanksgiving; he doesn't remember what he said at her funeral; and he doesn't remember Christmas the following month. I remember him as being lethargic at times. He was very intentional the day before and the day of Hannah's funeral. By and large, however, he did not seem to be emotionally present. This was the hardest part for me to watch. He seemed like an empty vessel, his heart buried six feet under where none of us could go with him.

I know my stepdad has always loved the older four of us, and even more so, he loves his grandchildren without an ounce of regret for the joy they bring. However, there is something about your own literal flesh and blood that makes the sting of death much more potent and permanent. His grief took on many forms over the following years, but the most interesting one is with how he cares for Hannah even in death. First it would be taking care of Hannah's dog who would live another three years; another was taking care of her final resting place.

The cemetery is a place of walking dead—people who have had their heart stopped but go to their loved ones' graves to try to find it's beat again. People crying by a grave are only understood by those who have been in that physical position before. A grave is a place of rest for the dead but a place of pain and peace for the living.

Where do you go to mourn if there is not a final resting place for your loved one? I imagine this could bring trauma and pain for people whose loved ones' bodies are missing—still out there somewhere in the world where no one can tend to their needs. The last thing we get to do for our loved ones is tend to their final resting place: bringing flowers, saying prayers, cleaning off hard water stains from the marble slabs. Having a place to go to mourn the loss of a loved one is essential for the family left behind. It is essential for a parent who has outlived a child and for a child who misses a parent. The body, although decomposing, or even cremated, is of great significance. The deceased loved one's presence is very real to those who are stuck among the living and the dead. This can only be understood by those who have gone through the same thing—the same pain and the same loss.

After a while of being in the emergency room, with hours until Hannah's body would be processed, I needed to do something. The doctor and nurses were so kind to allow us to stay the hours it took for her body to be retrieved. The cause of death at this point was unknown; all they could see were a set of parents, siblings, an aunt, and a set of grandparents in a room with their twenty-four-year-old loved one on a table with evidence of the paramedic's efforts to try and revive her. Even though Hannah's body was blue and cold to the touch, we could still hold Hannah's hands, move her limbs, and press our lips against her cheeks. It felt as if she were just asleep.

A thought occurred to me after several hours in the ER: the last time my mom had been home that day was when the paramedics carried Hannah off on a gurney to the ambulance and then to the hospital. I asked my mom if there was anything that needed to be cleaned up, because Hannah had vomited. Hannah's dog, Chica, also needed to be fed. My mom was shocked that I was willing to go to the house. I told her I wanted to. I didn't mention that I wanted to try to erase the stench of death from the living room.

Earlier in the week, Hannah had been prescribed codeine for a severe cold, and she'd texted her accountability group that she wanted to get high. She had not been tempted like this in a long time. She was proud of her three years' sobriety, but for some reason, that night, temptation got the best of her. The events that weakened her were unclear; what was clear in her text was that she drank the entire bottle of codeine.

A flood of emotions surfaced for us all. How could a bottle of codeine kill her? Was it for sure an overdose? Did she intentionally take more medicine to kill herself because she broke her sobriety? We shared the troubling news with my mom first, who in turn shared it with my stepdad. My mom started to weep, while my stepdad was puzzled. Hannah had done this before—tried to get high off of codeine—which was how she knew to do it. So what made this time so different?

Her exchange of texts seemed lucid and clear. She felt remorse and thanked her group for the encouragement. There didn't seem to be anything lurking in the background of the texts except the admission of drinking medication for the purpose of getting high, which had been a struggle for her in the past. She used to do drugs a lot to take her mind off of the pain she was in. But how exactly did she die?

Hannah was extremely overweight, so the amount of codeine given did not seem like it would be enough kill her. We would find out over the next week that these were the same questions the police needed to answer to figure out how and why she died. It would take another four months to get conclusive results returned to us by the coroner, who had the responsibility of declaring the cause of death. Specifically, we wanted to know what was in the toxicity report. How much codeine was in her bloodstream, and did that cause her death?

I hadn't really processed the idea that maybe I was going to a crime scene, doing my own investigation. It clearly wasn't a homicide to us, so cleaning up didn't seem like it was an issue in terms of a police investigation. Thankfully we found out that my trip to the Jacob Avenue house didn't cause any damage in that respect.

While I was there, I had another mission: find the codeine bottle. My mom said she saw it on the counter that morning, and it was full. Before my mom left for the gym, Hannah was asleep on the couch, and there was a full bottle of codeine on the counter. It didn't make sense to my mom why Hannah did not wake up when she returned an hour later.

The hospital was only ten minutes from my mom's house, and I needed a break from the despair in the ER. I arrived to find the scene as my mom had described it. The living room coffee table had been pushed to the side, presumably by the paramedics to get Hannah onto a gurney. There was some medical packaging left from the various devices used to try to revive her. I found the blanket Hannah had been sleeping under, and her pillow where the remains of her vomit had fallen. I stripped the pillow of its casing, and then I threw it and the blanket in the washing machine to clean the smell and the remnants of her last moments of pain.

Once I'd pushed the coffee table back into place and thrown the wrappings of medical equipment away, everything looked normal. I began to scour the counter for the medicine the doctor had prescribed for her severe cold. Sure enough: right there on one of the side counters in the kitchen was the orange-tinted plastic pharmaceutical bottle with the white cap and white label on it. Her name was there along with the drug name, "Codeine Sulphate Oral Suspension." And my mom was right: it was full.

When dealing with a drug addict, recovering or even sober, it's important to understand that they know how to cover their tracks. If Hannah had told her friends she drank all the codeine and yet the bottle was full, Hannah had to have filled it back up with something. I opened the bottle to smell it, not sure exactly what I was supposed to smell. Then I decided to pour a little in my hand to feel it, thinking that codeine should be a little thick or have a strong taste or smell to it.

The liquid that came out of the bottle had the consistency of water—and in fact, after sampling a small amount with the tip of my tongue, I concluded that it *was* water. To cover her tracks, Hannah had filled the empty bottle of codeine so my mom and stepdad wouldn't find out she had downed the entire thing. Hannah knew they would be upset, or maybe she just couldn't handle the disappointment in herself for breaking her three years of sobriety.

At first, it looked like Hannah's final act was one of guilt. However, she did confess to her accountability group. Hannah's final act was not taking the codeine or hiding it; it was her confession. Hannah died confessing her sins to her small group. In the week that followed, I would come to terms with this notion of her last confession as a point of peace for her. The last words Hannah read from her friends were of forgiveness and encouragement. Hannah's last words were not of a person who desired to end her life. These texts were a clue that would help in solving exactly what transpired between the hours of midnight and nine o'clock the next morning, when my mom found her.

If my parents heard her sleeping on the couch at eight o'clock, and my mom found her an hour later blue in the face from asphyxiation, what changed? How could my mom have missed saving Hannah by such a small window? Why hadn't Hannah's body exhibited symptoms of a drug-overdose earlier? These are questions my parents would fixate on for years to come and likely still do. The timing, the what-if questions, the blame my mom places on herself for leaving, the guilt that both my mom and stepdad were nurses and didn't know what had happened or was about to happen once they left the house that morning—these things still haunt them, some days more than others. For parents who lose a child, the what-ifs last forever. We are meant to outlive our children.

I know my own pain of losing Hannah, but seeing my parents suffer and be brought to their knees has been the hardest thing. I saw my parents as humans. The superheroes I had once idolized had fallen. The untouchable and unshakable force in my life had been bested by death's blow. It was difficult to watch. I would, however, spend the next years seeing them change from laid low to kneeling to standing to starting to take little steps again. The hardest part of seeing loved ones experience a loss is that you can't fix them. You can't make them run again. It almost invalidates the pain to expect them to do anything other than what they can do in any given moment. I didn't know it at the time, but I realized later that God used me, Katie, and our children to help my parents walk again. I don't think they'll ever run, but just seeing them walk means all the world. I know Hannah would be proud.

12

Prodigal Daughter

Funeral planning was where my ministry background kicked in. In ministry, there is a saying that we are in charge of "marrying them and burying them." Pastors train to walk alongside people through the highs and lows of life, and I knew what Hannah's church would provide. They would come through with funeral arrangements, pastoral care, and everything else we needed.

That Friday at the hospital, at some point in the chaos, I managed to talk to someone on staff at the church Hannah volunteered at and attended frequently. It was a big church close to our apartment, and I was expecting to talk to some random person who couldn't be expected to know the name of every member. Still, I knew contacting Hannah's church would relieve the burden of what to do next regarding arrangements for her funeral.

I introduced myself and said that I needed to inform the church of Hannah's death and ask for pastoral assistance. The lady on the other end asked in desperation, "Hannah Zeller is dead?" When she said Hannah's last name, I realized I must be talking to someone who knew her personally. As it turned out, the person who picked up the phone that day was Hannah's boss in the children's ministry.

My pastoral skills came in handy then as I walked her through the shock that I was in as well. I apologized for springing the information on her, and I just let her cry over the phone. She apologized for losing control of her emotions, and I told her, "It is meaningful to know that someone knows Hannah and is crying with us."

The lady said she would inform her children's ministry and contact the pastor of the young adult ministry. Hannah had spent the past year connecting with people her age in that ministry. The lady on the phone let me know that someone would get in touch with us. I also asked for a referral to a funeral home that would help us make arrangements for Hannah's body once we received it from the coroner's office.

Probably the two most long-lasting decisions were made that day by me. The first was deciding where the funeral would be held, which in turn decided who would perform the service. The second was choosing the funeral home, which was connected to a cemetery. What I didn't realize when the church referred us to the funeral home was that they also were referring us to Hannah's final resting place.

The funeral home got in touch with us the next day and set up a meeting on Sunday to make detailed plans. They assured us that they would be in touch with the coroner's office, and we would not have to do a thing. That was a relief. We had no idea what to do while her death was under investigation by the county. The funeral home said the body was always released within a couple days unless there was some extenuating circumstance to prevent it. Hannah's death wasn't a homicide, so all the evidence needed was at home or could be found in her blood.

The day after Hannah died was a Saturday, and we were all in shock. I knew that we needed to get ahead of the game on social media and control what we wanted to get out. Passwords for everything a person has is another huge challenge when someone suddenly dies. What was Hannah's password for Facebook and everything else? We still don't have the password to her Apple ID and can't fully transfer her purchased items off my mom's phone. Luckily, my mom knew where Hannah had written some stuff down, so we could gain access to her Facebook and manage what would be posted.

Before I showed up at the Jacob Avenue house Saturday, which was the place we would spend our time during the week with all the family coming into town, I had made an image for all of us to share. The idea was that we all write the same thing and post the same image at the same time. My mom had a verse she wanted. She found two pictures for us to choose from, and I edited the one we decided upon to the dimensions Facebook required at the time, so nothing would be cropped. The image would have Hannah's name, her birth date, and the date she died, along with the verse my mom wanted, 2 Timothy 4:7, "I have fought the good fight, I have finished the race, I have kept the faith."

This was a sibling group decision—to announce it together so that Hannah's friends and our family would know. All family members, including my mom's family and my stepdad's family, had been communicated with already, so we were confident this wouldn't catch any close relatives off guard.

The response immediately after we posted the image was amazing. We spent the entire day reading post after post from people who responded to each of our individual posts and the things they posted on Hannah's wall. It really was a good day to just sit and process and try to allow the reality of her death to sink in a little. I don't think it really did, but if anything, it was a calm before the next storm, which was having to make final preparations to say goodbye in a formal way.

The four remaining siblings each took on a different role in the decision-making process. My mom said later that she didn't know what she would have done without her four adult children making all the choices that she and my stepdad were unable to. I think it was how each of us siblings grieved; we wanted to help our mom and stepdad, but we also felt like we were helping and doing one last thing for Hannah.

My brother and his wife flew in sometime that weekend, and once the four of us were together it was different from what I'd expected. It really was not the same without Hannah around. There had been times when it was just the four of us growing up when we visited our father.

Hannah admitted during one of the sibling's wedding receptions that she struggled with our "other" life and family that she didn't get to be a part of. She was the oddball because it wasn't her family, it was the older four siblings' father's side of the family.

Yet when we were together that Saturday, the missing link was evident. Even her not being in the same room was evident. It was the first feeling of change—that things had shifted and would not go back to how they used to be. The permanency of death is the hardest part to overcome. There is nothing you can do to go back. You must move to a place of accepting a new reality, and even recognizing something is different is a hard step.

On Saturday, I realized I was the baby of the family again. There was no longer Hannah, my younger sister; it was me again as "little Diaz," just like I was in high school. Hannah was still in grade school then, so there was a whole other set of differences between what we called the "older four" and her. Our family dynamic was that I was the youngest in some settings, but in most times, Hannah was. I knew what it felt like to be the youngest, and it was a lot of how Hannah and I related earlier in our lives. But now there was only me.

Nothing changed for the other three in terms of family birth order. My brother was still the oldest, and the twins were still smack-dab in the middle. But I had become the youngest again. This was when the regret came back of how I had belittled Hannah as "younger," suggesting that somehow, I had more wisdom as the older sibling. Some of the tension I felt that week was in being treated as the younger sibling on top of realizing how I had treated Hannah unfairly on top of her death.

Saturday was a time of mental preparation for the rest of the week. On Sunday, we had our appointment with the funeral home. We did not realize this endeavor would last four hours, and that wasn't even the half of the planning that needed to be done. When we arrived at the funeral home, everyone who worked there was very calm and some somber as they talked with us. I could never work at a funeral home, dealing with grieving families day in and day out. It's the opposite of a promoter who always needs a smile on his face. At a mortuary, you always need to show the right amount empathy and sometimes sadness.

As a pastor, I always find it difficult to know what to say. My stepdad had taught me years earlier, when one of my students, Seth, passed away in an accident—one of Hannah's friends, as a matter of fact—to just say, "I am so sorry for your loss." I remember he hugged me that day as I cried, and he just repeated those words. I still say them to anyone I come into contact with who has lost someone. It really is the simplest, kindest way to affirm their grief.

A lot of people don't know what to say, and they end up saying the wrong thing. Never say something cliché to a grieving person, like, "At least they are in heaven," or "I know exactly how you feel." In the moment, I don't want them in heaven; I want them here. And no, you can't possibly know how I feel, because you are not me.

The poor lady who first came in to introduce herself made one of those "what not to say" blunders. You would think having worked at a funeral home, she would have come across this before. Perhaps we had set her up for failure or assumed she already knew our circumstances. My mom introduced herself and my stepdad, and then she introduced the four of us as her biological children. We just assumed she knew about how Hannah was related in the mix of children. My mom thought it was implied when she emphasized the four of us as being *her* biological children, but the words came out anyway: "So, did you two have any children of your own?" she asked my mom and stepdad with a face of true inquiry.

All our hearts sank. There was complete silence as if the giant elephant in the room was making all the noise for us. My mom just teared up and looked at my stepdad, who had this complete look of despair. The lady quickly realized her mistake and apologized profusely. I felt bad for the lady, but I guess my advice would be to know how the deceased is related to the family and to also understand last names. If someone ever mentions "biological children," it's implied there are some "not biological" children or siblings at play in the conversation.

There were so many decisions to be made, and we all had our own opinions of how it should go. Well, not all of us—our parents didn't care. We expected them to break the tie, but they were in too much shock to do so. We defaulted to narrowing down the options of things to two and asking Mom, "Do you want A or B?"

My stepdad didn't have the capacity to make any decisions. To choose two days after he lost his daughter what casket he wanted, what kind of encasing the casket should fit in when buried in the ground, or what plot of land we should pick was all too much. That last one was the curveball. We noticed driving up that the funeral home looked like a cemetery, and we'd wondered whether we'd have to decide where Hannah would be buried that day. I had just gone with the first funeral home recommended by the church based on who they had worked with before; it was close to the church, so it made sense. But to bury Hannah there was not a decision we had thought about.

I apologized to my mom for forcing her to more or less bury Hannah in a random cemetery basically because of logistics. It was close to the church for after the service but nowhere close to where they lived. My mom said it was okay; they wouldn't know of anywhere else to put Hannah except next to her grandpa up in the northern part of the city, but that was even farther from the Jacob Avenue house.

My family reassured me that it was okay, and it turned out to be a blessing to not have to find a cemetery to place Hannah in. It just made sense to look there, because there was no other option we felt like looking into. The funeral home ended up being perfect. My parents befriended our funeral coordinator, and she helped them over the years to manage Hannah's plot of land, taking care of the granite, and engraving, and making sure the grass was watered enough.

Thankfully, the four of us siblings are all very practical by nature. The casket was the least of our concerns. We wanted the low-grade, least-expensive, plane sturdy wooden box with no bells or whistles. One of the twins had the great idea of bedazzling the casket the way Hannah would all her books and knickknacks. We asked, "If we buy the casket, can we write on it and decorate it?"

The ladies helping us seemed a little surprised and said, "We don't see why not. It's yours, and it's going to be buried anyway, so go for it."

The idea was to get a bunch of different colors of duct tape, some of her favorite kinds, and turn the wooden box into something that was perfectly Hannah. This was our grief. We decided we wanted to celebrate all the things that made Hannah unique and different. Her million different colors of nail polish, the million different colors of hair dye she used over the years, her million different colored pens, her million different kinds of duct tape, and her millions of different random socks would all play into our week of planning. If we were throwing Hannah a surprise party, she would have loved it. That was our mind-set. We were preparing something special not just for Hannah but for us. We didn't care what anyone else thought. Our parents didn't care either way, so this was going to be a nontraditional service. It was going to be a Hannah-fied funeral.

Deciding on a plot of land was the last thing we wanted to do. Real estate for the dead is the same as real estate for the living: location, location, location. The good spots are near the fancy things, like monuments, buildings, and trees. The more affordable plots are located out where they just planted grass and a couple baby trees. None of us cared about the location, but my mom did want some shade. The place we could afford was right next to a baby tree, and she was hopeful that in time, it would provide more shade for Hannah's final resting place.

Everything in a cemetery is measured out to the exact inch, and there are markers or small numbered plaques in the ground that help you count which row and "seat" you were looking for, so to speak.

The plot we ended up with, completely by chance, was in row H. It was perfect for Hannah. There was only one other grave in use in the area at that time, but there would soon be more, and my mom would start to call them Hannah's neighbors. People who lose someone close and visit the cemetery often, become friends. My mom befriended the relatives of all of Hannah's neighbors over the years.

It is a kind and polite thing to check up on the neighbors' graves when you go to visit the cemetery. You pick up tipped-over flowers, rearrange fallen trinkets, throw away old flowers, and brush off headstones. Most importantly, if you are replacing flowers of your own that are still in good shape, you put them on a grave that doesn't have any. A cemetery can never have too many flowers or decorations.

We wanted plot H7 for Hannah because she was the seventh member of the family, but H5 was under the tree my mom wanted. We decided on H5 for Mom's desire for shade, because it really didn't matter to us. We also realized that Hannah was the fifth child, so the number five did have meaning after all. Hannah's final resting place was in a cemetery with the call number H5, in library terms. I took a mental picture of the marker that had H5 on it so I could remember how to count the columns and rows and find the exact location of my beloved sister.

H5, kind of by chance, or maybe out of our grief, became a mental marker for me. It became the location of an altar to God, to remember something that God had done in my life. It was Job in the Old Testament who cried out to God in worship when he found out his whole family had been killed, "The Lord gave and the Lord has taken away; may the name of the Lord be praised" (Job 1:26b). God was unfolding His larger story for me. He was piecing some things together that hadn't made sense until Hannah died. I would need these mental Instagram moments, and places, to preserve the lessons God was teaching me. H5 was more than her final resting place. It was her final volume in heaven's library.

God had taken my sister away along with the mystery of why I was living in a new city. He gave me a vision for my life that would be wrapped around the life and death of Hannah. He would give me a pedestal to stand on and speak truth into people's lives. In sharing the pain of my sister and in sharing my own pain, I would be able to share hope.

In Romans 8:23–25, we read:

> Not only so, but we ourselves, who have the first fruits of the Spirit, groan inwardly as we wait eagerly for our adoption to sonship, the redemption of our bodies. For in this hope we were saved. But hope that is seen is no hope at all. Who hopes for what they already have? But if we hope for what we do not yet have, we wait for it patiently.

If there was one chapter in the entire Bible to know by heart, Romans 8 would be at the top of my list. Paul brings together the crescendo of his sonata to the churches in Rome in this chapter. He bridges the gap of the entirety of humanity from past to present and into the future.

As believers, when another believer dies, we are forced in another direction. This direction is the future, eternity, a place where Jesus promises there is no pain or sorrow. It is a place where the living and the dead collide, a place I had never longed for until I realized my sister was there waiting for me. I discovered hope that this life is just a moment and on the other side of eternity awaits redemption, reconciliation, and restoration for all who call on the name of Jesus. As Hannah's story unfolded in the week between her death and her burial, her legacy would come together and be seared into my mind's eye.

Hannah was the walking embodiment of the prodigal daughter, but she spent the last year of her life safely home with both her earthly dad and her heavenly Dad, both of whom loved her and never gave up on her. The circumstances surrounding Hannah's death might make you think otherwise, but the reality is that there was no better time in her life to mess up and break her sobriety than in the arms of people who loved her and were willing to help her. Out of all the times Hannah slipped up, messed up, choked up, and gave up, the morning she died, Hannah had been in the best place emotionally and spiritually she had been in her entire life. I would rather Hannah died in those circumstances than during the years when she had wandered away from God.

What had changed to bring her back home? Hannah had finally understood that she could be broken and follow Jesus at the same time. She learned to allow God to use her, even though she felt useless on the inside. This transformation was the answer to the prayer my mom and stepdad had been praying since the Newsboys concert in Northern California a decade before. We didn't know that for Hannah's story to reach its apex and have its greatest impact, God would allow her to rest from this life and enter into the next. He could have stopped it, but we trust this mystery from a good God.

I never want to forget the vision of the altar God had given to me. I eventually had a logo designed after the grave marker and had it tattooed on my body. I carry her memory—in the marking of an altar God made for us—with me permanently now.

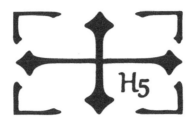

13

Years of Locusts

They placed a yellow flag on the cemetery plot with Hannah's name on it, the date she would be buried, and how far down to dig. We had two options: one was the depth to bury one person, the other was to dig twice as deep to be able to stack two cement casings. Each casing is of the exact size to place a casket in, so when they stack, there is actually a slab of cement separating them.

We asked why we had to pay for the cement casing, and they said it was to keep the ground level as things erode and deteriorate underground. It made sense. If a ton of holes were dug in a flat field and a wooden box placed in each one, over time, as the boxes broke down, the ground would sink in. However, at every cemetery, the grass is perfectly flat. The reason is that every casket is placed in cement box or upgraded to marble—for a price. Those materials don't degrade, and so the ground above them does not move.

When we first walked to the plot marked H5 and saw the yellow flag with Hannah's name on it, my older sisters began to cry. The reality was setting in that we were choosing where to bury Hannah's body permanently. That was something we'd never imagined we would have to do. We always thought that people, as they get old, buy a plot of land with their spouse and plan on being buried together. This was so out of the ordinary. A young death is hard to process.

I remember standing in the setting sun, looking around the

cemetery, and realizing that this would become a familiar place to us. Where Hannah is buried is where we go to talk to her. Everyone in the cemetery on any given day is there to talk to someone. It's a club that no one chooses to be in, as my mom continues to say.

We agreed to a full cement casing for the casket to fit into, and that was almost it for the day. We chose the cement over marble casing because it seemed like a meaningless extravagance to do anything above the minimal. We would never even see the cement or marble tomb; they sealed it up after the funeral once everyone had gone anyway. Maybe it was important to some people, but for us, it was just not Hannah and not affordable or necessary.

One of the other important decisions we had to make was what the headstone would be. At this particular cemetery, you could either have a flat headstone—which was a marble plaque on the ground—or what they called a bench. It was exactly what it sounded like: a giant granite bench designed for someone to sit on. It was engraved with birth to death dates and the name of the deceased, and we could add any special designs on different parts of the trim, top, and sides. We could even put a picture of our loved one on the front side of the bench. We were told it would last as long as the granite. My stepdad spoke up and said he wanted the bench. We didn't have any fancy stone for Hannah underground but we have nice granite in the spot that matters.

We decided that a picture would be nice to see—if it was as real and long-lasting as they promised. They said that the planning would have to be done on a different day, because it wasn't a necessity and would take months to order anyway. We said we did want to make the meeting sometime before the funeral, because all the siblings were in town, so they penciled us in for Tuesday evening.

Over the next forty-eight hours, we made decisions about that bench. We had several colors to pick from, some very intricate designs to make, and some verses to etch into the stone. This was where we wanted to put our time and effort. What would we be looking at every time we came to the gravesite? The bench was the memorial, just as much as knowing the placement of Hannah's body.

My stepdad spoke up again, only his second comment the whole day, when it came time to choose the color of the bench. He saw that there was a pink granite color and said, "It must be pink. Hannah's room was painted pink. She had her hair dyed pink several times. It's her favorite color, and I want to see pink when I visit her."

We couldn't argue with my stepdad's request. He hadn't said a thing but was very certain about the bench and the color. And so it was a pink stone bench we started making designs for.

It was for the best that my stepdad chose the color. After Hannah's death, he spent four-and-a-half years driving an hour from the northern part of the city down to the cemetery to visit Hannah every Sunday. My mom and stepdad would attend Hannah's church, then go to the bench, get lunch, and come home. It became a routine.

They started looking at how to protect granite from the hard water used to water the grass. Water spots were everywhere, and it bothered them. They started bringing a crate filled with many items—rags, brushes, toothbrush, spray cleaners of various kinds, dry towels, and a set of fake seasonal flowers they would rotate out monthly—along with a little step stool to sit on. They also bought lawn chairs and a giant beach umbrella that sticks into the ground. After my stepdad spent a half hour or so detailing Hannah's bench, they would sit there together.

I went with them a couple times to watch him work. I was fascinated by the way my stepdad's grief was playing out. He had found a niche—something that he would describe as therapeutic. There was a brush and spray for the granite, a different brush and spray for the engraved designs and lettering, and a third spray and rag to make Hannah's laser-printed picture sparkle.

After about a year, the black stain used for the photo engraving started to come off. My stepdad was frustrated, because they had assured us it would last for years, and the bench he was meticulously taking care of was degrading already. He went to talk to the cemetery office about it and received an apology. My parents decided to choose a white stain for all the engravings, and the cemetery officials paid for it. The white-stained letters and designs looked much better and have lasted much longer.

On top of taking such good care of the granite and the overall look of the bench, my mom would decorate it for everything. The Fourth of July, Easter, fall, Hannah's birthday, Christmas, spring, and summer flowers were the ones she came up with over the years. My mother sends me a picture every time she redecorates the bench to show me how it looks.

My stepdad works on his hands and knees caring for Hannah in death, and my mom focuses on how Hannah's bench is decorated, making sure it is always fashionable through each season. Even in death, my parents are still taking care of Hannah, and they will continue to do so for as long as they can walk. I don't think they will ever move away from this place; they could never leave Hannah unattended. I think it's how grieving parents deal with the death of their children. They still take care of them in some way, shape, or form.

There is an Ethiopian cross forever sketched in the stone of Hannah's bench to remind us that she was in the process of healing. It was also chosen to humble us. I judged Hannah for that cross on her chest. It was directly in the middle of her chest, protruding from her top shirt line. To me, it was another one of her attention-seeking behaviors. I think we all regret the judgment we passed on her. We never said anything bad about it, but I know I wasn't sincere when she first showed it to me. A lack of words is just as judgmental as words. Withholding affirmation is giving judgment.

None of us understood why Hannah got as many tattoos in random places as she did. To be honest, we were not a tattoo family, but there is usually one rebel in a family unit who wants to stick out. Either the whole family has tattoos, or there is just one.

It was odd to see this phase in Hannah's life, because I didn't understand why she would want to stick out more than she already did. Hannah even got a tattoo of footprints of her dog, Chica—her most faithful companion through the loneliest parts of her life—tattooed on her feet. She had the word *beautiful* etched on her shoulder in elegant cursive lettering. On her neck was a giant red rose with the words "Beautiful Mistake" written along the bottom.

The contrast between those two words defined Hannah's constant struggle. She wanted to see herself as beautiful but did feel like she was a mistake—the black sheep of the family. I think these carefully chosen words indicated Hannah's acceptance of herself. Hannah was broken, but she was okay. I think Hannah owned it in the end, realizing she wasn't supposed to be anyone other than who God made her to be.

Cornerstone Church in Chandler, Arizona, is a large church, and Hannah was so proud to be a member. She drove thirty to forty minutes from home three or more times a week to attend church, volunteer with children, go to Celebrate Recovery (a Christian-based addiction support group), and attend the young adult group. The young adult group and CR were exactly what Hannah needed. She had come a long way from one rough church experience to another rough church experience to finally finding one she felt comfortable in, one that embraced her unique style.

The last sermon series they were about to start was based off a book called *Weird: Because Normal Isn't Working* by Craig Groeschel. Hannah loved it and wore the shirt they had made with pride. The series reflected exactly how Hannah felt all the time: "Weird." The young adult pastor gave each of us family members a shirt as his memory of Hannah and how excited she was about the ministry overall.

Hannah's life was restored at that church, in her final year of living. It was worth the drive, because she was finally able to turn her hurt outward instead of inward and allow God to use her as he healed her. Hannah no longer believed she had to be healed before God would use her.

The night we planned her funeral at the church was beautiful and hard. We were incredibly encouraged to see this church come around us and love us, complete strangers to them, because of their love for our dear sweet Hannah. We had no idea of the impact she'd made in such a short amount of time. I realized that I'd missed what Hannah wanted me to see ever since they moved to the house on Jacob Avenue. I understood why she wanted me to go to the Halloween carnival; it was her home, and she'd wanted to show me she was okay.

One of my mom's favorite verses is Joel 2:25: "I will repay you for the years the locusts have eaten." God had sent over Israel a time of distress and famine to test them, but He promised He would not allow this to last forever. God restoring what was lost to the locusts was how my mom would describe redeeming moments in our lives. Hannah's last year of ministry at Cornerstone was God restoring years of pain and hardship she had endured.

I finally got a job after Hannah's death that will be my redeeming story. It is a good, steady job teaching teenagers the Bible in a loving community. My mom brought up Joel 2:25 again. In my previous job, I constantly felt unappreciated, held back from growth opportunities, blamed for mistakes not my own, and overlooked when chances for promotions were available. It was in this difficult period in my life of ministry that God refined me and allowed me to experience pain. The locusts were eating away at my spirit, and God knew that was happening, but he also knew where he was taking me.

I think it must have been a couple years into my new teaching job that I finally saw all the ministry opportunities I had. I realized that God had answered my prayers by taking me to a larger Christian organization. It just was not a church like I'd expected. My mom said to me in passing one day, when I was talking about the opportunity to speak at camp in front of more than four hundred and fifty people, "God is restoring the years the locusts have eaten, my son." As God had restored my sister in her last year of life, he began his restoration process in my life just weeks after Hannah's passing.

God had plans for me. God had brought me through a difficult five-year period to show me he had something better for me. It was most evident to me when the Spirit spoke into my soul the first summer the school sent me to Cambodia. In Cambodia, God showed me that he was restoring my lost time away from ministry and bringing me to an even greater ministry field.

In Cambodia, we worked with an organization called Rapha House that works with girls who have been rescued from sex trafficking. When asked about this trip, I explain that groups of teenagers go there every summer to experience and observe how God is healing these girls and restoring their brokenness. It is a very quick explanation, but as I fleshed it out, I realized my intent was to shake up my students, who appeared to sometimes be jaded by their Christian life. I wanted to take them to a place where we would find the worst parts of humanity, where evil was physically and spiritually present. I wanted to take them to the heart of darkness. There they could see the impossible: God working and his light shining through the lives of every person who worked with these girls and every girl who slowly allowed Jesus to shape her new identity.

Christianity is the only religion in which the cosmic creator God of the universe stepped down into history in the form of a man. This God-man, Jesus, experienced all our temptations and sufferings, and in spite of that, lived a perfect life, so that at the right time he could be offered as a perfect atoning sacrifice in place of our own broken lives. When that God-man was brought back to life by the power of the Holy Spirit, everything that God had intended to happen for humanity was fixed in the blink of an eye.

When the stone was rolled away and Jesus was not in his tomb, there were several simultaneous ramifications. He conquered death, which foreshadows our own victory over death. It wasn't just our sins that were forgiven by his death on a cross, it was a new life we were given. Paul says to the Romans, "If the Spirit of him who raised Jesus from the dead is living in you, he who raised Christ from the dead will also give life to your mortal bodies because of his Spirit who lives in you" (Romans 8:11). It proves that there was access to life here and now.

Why did Jesus walk among the people for forty days after he was resurrected and not just a day? That was to demonstrate God's perfect amount of time to show there is life to be given here and now, not just in the age to come. Jesus started his ministry being tempted in the desert for forty days, and for forty days he would end his ministry proving he conquered death.

When people come to the Lord—when they hand over their pain, brokenness, shame, hurt, sin, guilt, and anything that is a result of being a human in a fallen world—Jesus scoops it all up as if these are clothes and puts them on himself. No matter the weight of it all, he is strong enough to wear it for us. In place of those ragged, tattered, heavy clothes, he gives us a new identity. He gives us his clothes that are pure white, light, and perfect, "… since you have taken off your old self with its practices and have put on the new self, which is being renewed in knowledge in the image of its Creator" (Colossians 3:9-10). The Holy Spirit, the same Spirit who brought Jesus back to life, comes and dwells inside of us who have professed our faith in Christ. That process of regeneration, justification, and sanctification is something that only God can do.

This is the same conclusion Hannah came to in her last year of life. She spent nine years in darkness among well-intentioned but abusive people, including myself—people who looked at her, judged her, and treated her as somehow weak for straying. Christianity in America can be very unforgiving to those who have grown up in the church. This is why pastors' and missionaries' kids have it so tough; people look at them, point to their parents, and say, "You are supposed to look like them. What's wrong with you for messing up?"

Those of us who have grown up in the church are looked to as people who should know better and not do all the bad things we've been warned about. It really is the story of the prodigal son. There arc those who lose their way for a time, and there are those who have never left. In the parable, the one who stands in judgment is the brother who never left. He is jealous of his father's forgiveness offered to the brother who sinned. I think it is safe to assume that this story is not just about two individuals and their father; it's about all of Christendom. The older brother represents all of us who self-righteously think we deserve more because of our faithfulness.

We tend to look at our broken brother or sister and say, "We are the same. We both know right from wrong. We had the same upbringing, but I stayed the course." We say in judgment, "Why can't you do what I have done? Why should I show you grace when I had the same temptation and decided not to give in to it? You did all these things to yourself by leaving our father's household." Jesus's point with the parable is that the older brother has the exact same blessings as the younger son who ran away. However, the older brother refused to forgive; more than that, he refused to celebrate a sinner's repentance.

This parable shows our own true brokenness and works-based mentality. The older brother thought his devotion made him greater, but the father's love for both sons was equal the entire time. The father made the point to the older brother that the younger brother had to learn the hard way, but the older brother was safely in his house with all its blessings the whole time. Those of us who have been in our father's household, who have learned to stop wandering, need to constantly do the work of our father and look for our brothers and sisters who are far off but are trying to make their way home. We should be yelling from the rooftop, "Come home!" When they get back home, we should never say, "You left, and all this pain you did to yourself." We should embrace them with unconditional love and be joyful that our brothers and sisters in Christ who lost their way are now safe again.

Hannah seldom felt that welcome-home embrace from churches and communities throughout her life. There were small pockets of friendship, including a small-group leader who was our cousin. There were church services and ministries Hannah enjoyed, where she thirsted for more of God in her life, but there wasn't a complete embrace of all parts of her. As she was feeling rejected by churchgoers, I added to her pain by being another person who held her to impossible standards. My reasoning was, *Why did you stray? I stayed. You did this to yourself.*

When Hannah moved back from Colorado, she tried to tell me that she had come home. It started in the rental house before Jacob Avenue; she found a church where she got involved in the children's ministry for the first time. Hannah had always gone to church as a consumer—a broken person needing healing—but something changed when they moved. Hannah realized her love for children, or maybe God just placed it in her heart. This was Hannah's first time joining a ministry team. Instead of waiting to be accepted, she sought out a place to serve, and within that, she found community. That short time in the rental house gave her a vision of what to find when they ended up in the house on Jacob Avenue.

During their process of moving out of the rental house and into the Jacob Avenue home, Katie asked around for suggestions of larger churches that had amazing worship, because that is what Hannah loved most. For some reason, Katie felt called to contact a friend from college about her church, which was in the east valley. It sounded exactly like the past churches Hannah had been to in terms of style, Katie suggested that Hannah check it out.

When Hannah first attended a service at Cornerstone, she knew immediately that it had the style of music she loved, a crowd that was unashamed to worship outwardly, and worship style that had a rock edge to it—the kind where you can feel the bass and the drum kick. Hannah had picked up some tools on her journey to the house on Jacob Avenue that she knew she needed in her life for self-care. She applied to volunteer and was accepted into the children's ministry. To serve and find Hannah's purpose instead of just seeing herself as broken or not useful to God was a sign of her identity starting to change.

Hannah knew she needed accountability for her past vices, and so she joined Celebrate Recovery at the church with a group of girls she felt safe confiding in. This propelled this transformation process even more. She loved the young adult pastor's preaching and his style; he had a long beard and tattoos, and it was this misfit pastor that she immediately identified with.

The young adult ministry would put on random events that she loved to go to. Her last one was an eighties dance party, where she decked herself out in the proper getup and hairdo. In the pictures of that event, you can see a beaming smile, something I hadn't seen on her in a long time. That is what I missed and have since learned or been reminded of. Hurting people's final road to recovery is to find their ministry again. God's plan is not to leave you in your brokenness but to show you how to serve others despite your imperfection.

Paul says this same thing when he mentions some "thorn in my flesh" that he pleaded for Jesus to remove. Whether it was a physical ailment (which many scholars think it was), a person antagonizing him or spiritual oppression, Paul still served faithfully. Jesus said to

Paul, "My grace is sufficient for you, for my power is made perfect in weakness" (2 Corinthians 12:9). Paul learned that when we serve God despite any pain or bad circumstance, Jesus provides the perfect amount of grace we need—no more and no less.

Hannah learned to serve. She learned to give of herself willingly and not wait for her pain to subside. Part of healing from pain is allowing God to use you and relying on his strength, not your own. If you are saved by faith, you are also sanctified by faith. You must trust that even though you don't feel useful to God, he can still use you. In fact, he has promised that you were created to do good works (Ephesians 2:10). It is in your DNA to do God's kingdom work. God restored many lost years in Hannah's life—nine years in one year. She was the prodigal daughter.

14

A Forced Goodbye

I put a lot of pressure on myself the week after Hannah died to make the perfect movie for her funeral. It was going to be my way of honoring her. By Wednesday night, I broke down and asked my brother for help. He was the hip engineer who taught himself how to be an actual DJ with two turntables and a microphone. He taught himself Apple Logic, the powerhouse of audio recording and editing. Music editing or even sound effects in any video is half the video, and people don't always pay attention to that part of the process. What makes a good movie is the music and sound effects. What makes a video look professional is not only a better camera but actual audio equipment.

I knew that my brother had the same attention to detail that I had and could easily make the video. I asked him if he could take on the project, because I was burning the candle at both ends. I worked three days and was still having to wake up in the middle of the night to help Katie nurse Emi. She was now almost five pounds but still under the seven pounds the doctors wanted her to be at before we could let her sleep through the night. I had reached my end and needed to let go of the thing I wanted to do the most.

Fortunately, my brother and his wife rocked it. They had to pick out all the pictures and then convert them to digital copies. I was going to scan them with my own scanner, but my brother's wife said it would be faster to just let FedEx do that for us. That was a novel concept. I didn't know FedEx did that.

My brother had brought his own MacBook Pro so he could make the movie the way I'd intended. I said, "I know I'm asking you to do a lot at the last minute,and I really have no place to tell you how to do this, but please don't make a PowerPoint slideshow video." He laughed; he knew exactly my issue and had the same feeling. This wasn't a business meeting or video of summer camp. It was the story of our sister. It was a perfect addition to the funeral. My vision for the funeral was that I wanted to start with the video.

The second vision I had for the funeral was to extend an invitation to all to follow Jesus by showing how Hannah was a disciple of Jesus. Before discipleship, extending the invitation to repent and turn to Jesus is given. It's interesting that we as a church are okay with offering salvation to all but not discipleship to all. I think Hannah understood this need for discipleship more than most people. She was hurt by this idea that only some people got attention for discipleship. She would rededicate her life to Christ because that is where everyone celebrates. Somehow, we humans fail to see discipleship, and celebrating that is just as important.

We do not get to play God and only save and disciple a few. If we extend salvation to all, we must extend the invitation of discipleship to all. Hannah was often ignored because she was not one of the popular ones. She was forgotten at different points in her life and scarred by different churches along the way.

Would you rather disciple a popular kid who has no spiritual depth and no desire to be transformed or a kid who is "different" but does get it and grows deeper in the walk because of you? I'll pick the "different" kid every day. That is who my sister was and who I was called to and who I still seek out.

The excuse that I often here is, "I can't possibly disciple every single kid who comes through my door." The reality is that not everyone wants to be discipled by you, but if you don't extend the invitation to disciple everyone, you are not following Jesus's model. We read in John 6:66 that many of his disciples turned back and no longer followed him because his teachings were too hard. We know for sure that twelve disciples remained. One of them, Judas, was a wolf in sheep's clothing. Jesus had more than twelve; we guess potentially a few thousand were following him at this point, and they chose to leave.

As well, Jesus was working with grown adults. We do not get to select only twelve children to disciple. My argument in selective discipleship with teenagers and younger is that you are hindering them from coming to Jesus. You are putting a stumbling block of sin in front of them, and we have already discussed this offense (Matthew 18:6). As a Christian, no matter your position, when you are mature and are ready to disciple others, you must extend the invitation to all, then see who remains. You could save a life—or quite possibly hinder your own.

There must be a better way to run a church. The current way of doing things hurt my sister and twisted my view of God. I felt that I had to do the work of sanctifying myself instead of realizing that I must allow the Holy Spirit to do that. Only God can save us, and only God can change us. That was the missing component in my theology and Hannah's, but the ironic thing is that Hannah learned this years before me, the ordained pastor.

At Hannah's viewing, I almost lost control of my senses. Seeing her embalmed body was a thousand times worse than seeing her on the hospital bed. Hannah was very clearly not there anymore. Her face was dolled up and her hair was straightened. I don't know how my older sisters emotionally handled preparing her body. Hannah was unmistakably dead and very eerily asleep. This was not my Hannah, and this was not what I had expected to see or feel.

As my wife and I approached the final resting bed of my sister in the funeral home's viewing room, I heard people to my left talking and whispering. I was angry. Why is there small talk in a place where we are supposed to come to grips with the stark reality of Hannah's death? I needed to process this, and I couldn't in such a mixed environment of clichés and unfitting attitudes. My heart dropped; I wanted to cry, but my pride would not allow me to. I was either going to vomit or pass out from the confused feelings—or possibly from my suit shirt, which barely fit my neck and was not allowing me to take a deep breath.

As we reached Hannah, the first thing I noticed was her jawline. It is the one thing that never quite looks right on a person who has been embalmed. The skin is pulled down because the neck is propped up and gravity has taken its toll. Her nose was still slightly discolored at the tip, that makeup could not fix. Trying to make a dead person look alive just seems odd. It's as if we are afraid of death and need to hide its presence. I would take hiding death behind a white cloth over pretending death was not there at all. At least hiding the body is still recognizing that person is dead, and it is admitting that we do not want to see our loved one in that state.

Embalming seems backward. Your last memory of a loved one is a preserved version of the dead body—a wax museum figurine. Thinking back to my grandma Carmen's viewing, she also looked fake, and I wish I didn't remember her that way. Her hands were stiff, and her face was droopy. I had attributed my memories of the plasticity of her prepared body to old age. I had prepared myself for the opposite—that Hannah was so young she would not look plastic. I was mistaken.

I don't like having to hide from death, and I didn't like having to see my sister in her casket, with the lighting set so low and the soft music in the background. It was perhaps the first time I felt the reality of her death. In the hospital, her blood was still providing some sign of life or at least recent life. There was the illusion of hope that she might still come back to life. It wasn't set in stone; maybe a doctor could come in and do something. There in the funeral home, it was permanent. My sister was dead, and I was being forced to accept a world without her in it. I was being forced to say goodbye, and I could not.

What did not help my attitude in that moment was the chatter. It was the people talking—paying no attention to my sister, ignoring her like we so often had—it made my stomach drop. Maybe that was the most difficult part. As a family, we had often carried on conversations with her in the background or in the other room. Sometimes she would join in, and other times she would not. Her depression would often get the best of her, and she found that isolation was her only companion (that and her dog, Chica). In that moment, approaching her open casket with no one standing by to give her the attention she deserved, I couldn't give her the respect I wanted to. So, I turned around and left.

I looked at my wife, said I was sorry, and headed for the back door. As I hurriedly walked down the aisle to the rear exit, I briefly saw my mother out of the corner of my eye—saddened not for my leaving but for my grieving and knowing it was too much for me at that moment. Once I made it outside, the tears came. But it is more than just tears that accompany the cries of a person mourning; it is the pulled-back face and elongated smile that allows for a deep and uncontrollable burst of noise from the depths of the diaphragm. As I allowed myself to cry for a moment and catch my breath, I began to process my new reality. Hannah was gone, and the body in that casket was just a shell, as my brother had described it earlier that day.

I took off my suit coat and tie and unbuttoned the collar that had been choking me. I stood there for several minutes in a daze. I was not prepared for the feelings that had transpired in that room. I don't know what I was expecting, but that was not it.

Hannah had asked us the previous January if we could have a little girl for her birthday that April. My wife and I both rolled our eyes at her and smirked, knowing that we could neither control the gender nor would we have a baby because she wanted us to. Little did Hannah know at the time, we were trying to have a third child and were secretly praying for a little girl. I was praying for a little girl because I was afraid that if we had another boy, in two years we would be in the same spot trying for the fourth child—that magical girl every mother wants.

On Hannah's birthday, we had her close her eyes, and my wife placed the pregnancy strip in her hands. When Hannah opened her eyes, she stared at the strip confused for a second. But as soon as she realized what had been placed in her hands, who had placed it there, and the secret the item revealed, she screamed. I had never seen Hannah more excited, with the biggest grin on her face, at the fact that we were having not just another child but a girl.

Hannah was always the biggest fan of my wife and I having children. Hannah loved my three children with more compassion and heart than I ever have felt for someone else's children. We have another girl now, and she has the exact same eyes and complexion as my sister. Hannah would be ecstatic.

Hannah immediately began all the girly projects she had been planning. One of them was a painting for the nursery that she gave to us at the baby shower. It was hand painted with these words: "She knew that she was formed in God's hands, dreamed up in His heart, and placed in the world for a purpose." I found this quote later credited to a Twitter account with the name @Godposts. I would never have guessed that Hannah's words to my baby girl, her niece, would come to be the most profound statement about herself.

The painting was propped against a few boxes in the nursery, and I hung it up the night Hannah died. My little girl will never know my sister personally, but she will hear stories and feel the love Hannah had for her even before she was born. Whenever I look at my beautiful little girl, I will always be reminded of Hannah. I will see the grin of excitement Hannah had when we found out God had blessed us with another child. I will always remember those two months. My daughter came into this world in mid-September, and my sister left this world about two months later. Hannah had two months to hold and love the precious girl she had prayed for. I am convinced we had a girl because Hannah specifically prayed for it.

I made my way back into the lobby, and moments later, my stepdad walked in the room and asked if I was ready to go see Hannah again. He wanted to go with me and be by my side. He told me that he wanted to make sure I said my goodbyes that night at the viewing, because there would not be time the following day at the funeral service. We had speaking parts to prepare for and needed to be in the right emotional state to deliver them. I asked my wife if she would join me also, and she grabbed my hand and walked with me. The three of us made our way down the aisle—not at all the aisle we would have wanted for Hannah.

My mom described the week of Hannah's preparations as the wedding we never got to have. My mother noted all the similarities between wedding planning and funeral planning. Everyone needed nice outfits. We had to pick out flowers. We met with the church and planned a service. We needed a nice outfit for Hannah. My older sisters wanted to do her makeup and nails.

I give my older sisters so much credit for being able to touch Hannah post-embalming. I would not have been able to spend time in the room with Hannah at that point, much less prepare her body. They spent a couple of hours doing everything you would do for a bride on the day of her wedding. They did Hannah's hair, her nails, her makeup and chose her outfit. As the women in the Bible would take spices to prepare the bodies of their loved ones who died, my sisters were honoring Hannah in that same manor. My older sisters sprayed perfume on Hannah, a spice. I think the process was healing for them.

The other similarities to a wedding were that we had to be at certain places at certain times, and we had to communicate to everyone the times of the service and viewing. Family flew into town and drove into town from all over the country. It felt like we planned a wedding in a week. The only difference, besides the obvious, was the coloring—black instead of white.

It united us as a family, knowing we had all pitched in to give our sister the attention and "wedding" that she never got to have. We spent several thousand dollars, as much as any average family would on a wedding.

The second time I approached my sister in that room was the same. I could hear people talking and ignoring my sister. However, instead of leaving, I turned around and asked if people could stop talking for a few moments while I said goodbye to Hannah. To my amazement, all twenty or so people in the room apologized and left the room, shutting the doors behind them. I did not mean for them to leave, but the privacy surprisingly helped.

It might be a guy thing. We don't usually like crying in front of people. I did not want people to watch me in my last moments with my sister. With my stepdad on my right and my wife on my left, I stepped up to where Hannah lay. Her hands were stiff. I knew what to expect now. Her body was no different from what I had experienced with my different sets of grandparents. My head began to sway, and the tears came rushing out.

I buried my head into my stepdad's chest and wailed. My heart ached. My eyes quivered, and my noises were uninhibited. I was finally able to put sounds to what my body was feeling, and what my mind was deciphering.

I repeatedly said to my stepdad, "This isn't her. She isn't here."

He hugged me and squeezed me, and with his own cry, he said, "I know, baby. I'm so sorry." He had called all of us "baby" at one point or another throughout our lives, but I had never heard it the way he said it now. He completely empathized with me and carried me in that moment. I was a grown man and still in need of protection by a faher figure.

I will never forget saying goodbye to my sister with the two people I needed the most with me. I didn't regret seeing Hanna's body after that. It was precious. We may have been hiding death from ourselves, but we were more importantly preparing her for her final resting place. I suppose it is respectful and honoring to bury the dead in the same manner that we would treat them if they were alive. No one wants to leave their house unkept or go to church not in their Sunday best, not looking proper. It is the same with our dead. We honor and respect them both physically and emotionally.

15

Happenstance

The most accumulated rainfall in one day in the valley in eighteen years occurred on the day we laid my sister to rest. I would not have had it any other way. There is something spiritual, something inviting, something poetic, something memorable, something soothing about a funeral on a cloudy, rainy day. When it's a wedding day, we hope for the best weather but for a funeral, the rain was welcomed. We had planned for it—rain had been forecasted earlier that week—and we bought our own umbrellas. We arrived at the church, and the hearse had already arrived. My stepdad helped the funeral home staff get the casket out of the hearse and onto a cart with wheels. My wife was gracious enough to drop me off at the front so I could help bring Hannah's casket inside the church.

We carried her to a side room where we did a second viewing. The Thursday viewing was a private invitation for extended family only. We decided we wanted friends to be able to see her one last time. What bride wouldn't want to be seen two days in a row in all her getup?

I was hesitant to go in there. I wanted my head clear for what I was going to say, and I felt that I had already said goodbye two times and would do so a third at the cemetery. What I was really looking for were Hannah's friends from our hometown—the fellow misfits she had stayed in touch with when she moved to Colorado, her concert buddies who I would drive hours through the night to get us home.

God had put it in my heart that they needed me to be Jesus to them. Somewhere they had lost their way, and if I was courageous enough, on behalf of Hannah, I could extend an open invitation. As I looked in and said hello, I saw so many old friends who drove the almost three-hour trip from our hometown to Hannah's church. But I didn't see the ones I was looking for.

As with our Facebook post, the response was overwhelming. All these people had come because their lives had been touched by Hannah, or they knew the pain our family was in and wanted to support us through it. We knew there would be both believers and unbelievers, and we wanted to take the opportunity to share the Gospel as clearly as possible. The young adult pastor—the one with the beard and tattoos who Hannah loved—was officiating, and we told him that if we hadn't already shared the Gospel enough in our own speeches, he needed to bring it home for us.

At some point, the side room was open to just our family and grandparents. We were all standing in front of the casket with only candles for light. The funeral directors were there too, along with an assistant. We all held our breath, knowing the next step was the funeral service. I could not predict that this would stand out as a defining moment—the beginning of the end of the goodbyes that had been going on an entire week.

The funeral home assistant closed the lid of the casket, stuck a large metal tool into a small hole I hadn't noticed, and twisted until we heard the loud "clank" of the casket being locked. It almost echoed, and time stopped abruptly. What had just happened? The funeral home had warned us of this, but we could not prepare for that sound.

Almost simultaneously, my family began to weep and wail. That sound was death's knock at our door. It solidified the fact that we would never see her again. The sound was soul-wrenching. I could hear it and feel it in the cries of my family. Closing the lid and locking it permanently was the end, and we felt its echo.

What had we done? Could we open it one more time after? Could we see her one more time at the cemetery? Why did it have to be this way? We'd been warned that once the casket was locked, it would remain locked and be buried locked. Why did I remain quiet? I am not sure. I was still numb, and I was also focused on what I would say during the service. My heart felt the knock, but it did not make the connection to my tear ducts.

We thought we were in the side room in private, but my mom's sister, my aunt, would later tell us that everyone could hear our cries echoing from the room, even as they sat in the sanctuary of the church. She described it as bittersweet; everyone was sad for us but felt it was an honoring way for the funeral to start, a very unintentional way on our part.

We walked Hannah down the church aisle—another wedding moment—and we spent the next hour and a half not only honoring her but recognizing the presence of God in our family, in Hannah's life, and in the lives of anyone who wanted His presence. In her death, we had to offer life to others. What else could her death mean except to serve to further the kingdom? Hannah devoted her final days to this calling with children, and we wanted to do the same.

Watching the opening movie montage of pictures of our sister as a baby and slowly growing up was hard, but it was necessary to allow us to recognize what exactly we had lost. Hannah wasn't just anyone—she was a daughter who was once a baby who grew up. She was a sister who looked up to her four siblings. She was a friend who smiled and laughed at all things weird. At each stage of her life in the video, someone in the audience could point out a memory. All of those gathered were included in the memory of her, no matter how long it had been since they saw her. It drew them in, allowing them to feel our sorrow and loss.

We wanted people to leave having been moved from sorrow to hope. We had some good friends from our hometown drive down to sing a couple of worship songs. This couple would later form a band called Tow'rs. As husband and wife duo band was just starting out, one of the twins reached out to them to lead us in worship. When she said their names, I knew instantly they could pull off what my mom most wanted.

The song "Oceans (Where Feet May Fail)" by Hillsong United had recently come out and had just started being played on the radio the month prior. The vocals on the song are amazing, but in a very high octave toward the crescendo of the song, and our friends nailed it. It was the song that carried us through the next year.

"Oceans" references the story of Peter walking on the water as an act of faith to walk toward Jesus who was standing there in a storm waiting for him. The words to the song expand the story of Peter and Jesus to encapsulate the full meaning of that passage of scripture. It's about trust. It's about fear. It's about uncertainty. It's about the unknown. It's about believing what you can't see. It's about moving forward. Most of all, it's a prayer to God—a prayer telling Him you are willing to go even into failure and fear because you have faith.

After the song ended, the twins each read a verse. My brother gave the eulogy, and I spoke about what had changed her life. I felt it was important for everyone to know what was different about Hannah now versus Hannah from ten years ago. I gave a sermon on what changed within Hannah. What I had missed in my years of judgment, as I reflected now on her life, was her growth. She had moved from someone who relied on everyone else to carry her emotionally and spiritually to a person who realized that God had another way to heal her.

You can stay stuck in your brokenness and self-pity, or you can serve God and allow him to heal you along the way. Hannah realized that serving gave her the purpose she was searching for, which in turn healed some of her hurts and pain. She learned the mystery of gratitude. When people come to Christ and understand what they have been saved from, they should feel gratitude toward God. People who are thankful toward God will serve Him even if they are broken. They won't sit around waiting for someone to fix them, because they understand that God has given them a calling, a purpose, and that God will fix them along the way.

Hannah realized that maybe the reason she was in a constant downward spiral was because she was waiting to be fixed before she experienced the joy that comes through serving God with your life. You can be both broken and pursuing God at the same time.

The night before Hannah died, my stepdad had to get up for work early, so he couldn't finish watching the Avalanche hockey game with her. Hannah moved to the living room couch to finish the game. At one point before he fell asleep, Hannah ran into my mom and stepdad's room and exclaimed, "There was a great fight, with blood on the ice!" The best part of watching hockey is that they can punch it out for a while. The suspense of the game was nil, because the Avalanche were losing, but that fight was enough to get Hannah up and running to tell her dad about it. He was supposed to stay up and watch the game with her like he had done from time to time, but he was tired that day. He regrets not watching that last game.

Is this chance? Is this bad luck? Is this the way fate plays out? Sometimes you win some and other times you lose some? Is it wrong to think that something greater than ourselves allows it? Which scenario is worse: a mistake, a slip-up in the heavens, that death went to the wrong house? Or, that God knew what would happen, saw it from the beginning her end, and stood idly by (or so it seems to us)? Does God force people to do things? No. Could he stop some things? Yes. Would he allow someone to die through a series of human choices? Yes. Why, why would he allow all this pain? Why do some people get to live while others die? Why do good people suffer, and wicked people prosper? I'm beginning to sound like the Psalmist who makes the same proclamation: "This is what the wicked are like—always free of care, they go on amassing wealth" (Psalm 73:12).

Our questions are nothing new. They have been asked of God for thousands of years. The problem of death is that it is the greatest mystery to us because there is no cure for it. Why do Christians proclaim that Jesus was resurrected? Why is this an imperative? It's essential, outside of our biblical and theological arguments, for Him to defeat death because it's the one thing we don't know for certain what happens after we experience it and the one ailment for which we will never find a cure.

It goes back to time: God's idea of time and our idea of time. Everyone is going to die—everyone. No one lives in this life forever. When we ask questions of God that have to do with death, for him time is irrelevant because he is not confined to time like we are. He both sees Hannah the moment she died and then sees her the moment she reached the other side of eternity. We think there is suffering, and indeed there is potential suffering if you don't believe in God, because God's word says that you must have faith that God exists and that he rewards those who earnestly seek him and find him in Jesus (Hebrews 11:6). When someone dies, it does not surprise God. It is the state of a person's soul that matters most. If as Christians we don't know when, but we know what can bridge this life to the life to come, then we should care more about the living.

We can ask God why and accept Him, allow His healing touch, reach out to Him in our depth of pain. Just because we are hurting, and we have this inkling that God knew about it and allowed it, doesn't mean we push Him away. We embrace Him, for it is far better for someone to die for a purpose than for life to be one big cosmic accident. After all, Hannah could have died at so many points on the road of her life. Five years prior she was at her lowest point, suicidal and cutting herself to ease her pain. She would find boyfriends to sleep with looking to find love in those broken relationships.

When Hannah died the morning after the hockey game, there was nothing out of the ordinary for my parents to notice. Hannah was on the couch. She had covered her face with a pillow as she usually did to block the sun. She was snoring loudly, and her chest was moving up and down. My parents wish they would have checked on her; all they would have needed to do was move the pillow to see the beginning signs of her body shutting down. Hannah's skin would have been cool to the touch. Her lips would have started to turn blue. She might have already vomited, and she would not have responded to them trying to wake her up. But both my mom and stepdad decided to let her sleep in.

My dad always goes to work, so that wasn't out of the ordinary. My mom does a variety of things. For some reason, that morning she decided to leave the house and go to the gym to work out. She did the same thing she would have done any day of the week, whether Hannah was asleep on the couch or in her room. My mom wouldn't need to check on her when Hannah was on the couch, but if Hannah had been in her room, my mom might have checked on her more closely. Since she was out on the couch, they could see her just enough and hear her. She appeared very much alive when my mom left, and her codeine bottle looked as it did the night before.

Why did Hannah have to leave it out with water to hide that she drank it all? Why didn't she just hide the bottle? Was it her own fault for trying to hide her mistake? Was death her punishment for that? We would find out later that there was more than just codeine in her system. Still, had it been the correct dosage of codeine her normal doctor prescribed, knowing she had a history of drug abuse, she might still be alive. Instead, a different doctor prescribed one of the more potent dosages. If the codeine had not been so potent, all the other factors would not have caused her overdose. Hannah shouldn't have had that amount available to her to begin with.

Why was my mom gone the amount of time she was? Why did she leave at the exact time she did? There was a one-hour window, and my mom returned home just minutes after Hannah stopped breathing? Why couldn't she have been gone all morning, and then the proximity of time wouldn't have mattered? Why couldn't she get home faster? Why were there the number of cars on the road that there were? Why did she drive the speed that she did? Why, why, why, why?

All the scenarios are the same. It might as well have been a car accident, Hannah getting hit by a drunk driver or falling asleep at the wheel, or maybe drowning in a swimming pool. We will still ask why.

What could we have done to prevent it? It's hard to escape the guilt of thinking you could have done something to stop it from happening. We may never have a sufficient answer to *why*, but we can address the issue of guilt.

Guilt is the burden of death. Guilt makes you believe that you are at fault for what happened. If everything is one big happenstance, accident, or bad luck, then the burden of death, the weight of guilt, rests heavily on your shoulders. You, in theory, could have turned left when you should have gone right. You could change the outcome of anything on one hand or blame yourself for what you caused. When you take God out of the equation and everything is up to the "universe" to decide, then our lives are almost devalued. Death is meaningless, and therefore life is meaningless in and of itself. One can create meaning for life, but death nullifies it.

One purpose for life, a person can believe, is to enjoy it to the fullest. Focus on self and indulging in pleasure, because who knows—tomorrow we might die. On the other end, you might try to avoid death, cheat death, and escape the ever-creeping marks of time wrinkling your skin. You make yourself younger, you make yourself stronger, you invest your life in preserving this life in order to avoid death at all costs. Life becomes about *you*. You either become a hedonist living for pleasure or you become a preserver. You store up things as if you can outlive the coming apocalypse.

Even the healthiest people are stricken with diseases and die. Even the wealthiest are in accidents and perish. Death shows no favoritism. Death is not prejudicial or racist. Death can happen at any time, at any place. It is happening right now. It is estimated that there are two deaths every second of every day worldwide (http://www.ecology.com/birth-death-rates/). We can't avoid talking about death, and some deaths can seem insignificant to people. However; if the dead could speak, I think they would tell us, "Do something." Don't spend your life in guilt if you do not know how much time you have. For the Christian, life and death are so much more.

For a long time in our US history, the focus of our faith has been salvation. You need Jesus because you need to be saved. You want to avoid going to hell? If time is relative, then those questions don't matter to God. Once you're saved, he isn't wandering around hoping that it all pans out in the end for you.

What if salvation is just the beginning of our lives? What if the reason Jesus left and sent the Holy Spirit is because for the first time, God was able to do what He was planning on doing, which was to be intimately involved with his creation? He can walk with us again in the cool of the day as He did in the garden. People who are walking, breathing torchbearers of the King go out into the world and bring light to the darkest corners of the earth. Does God do great things? Always! Does God love using his people to do great things? Always! You can live life for *you*, or you can step into the unknown and see what exactly this great thing is that God wants you to do.

One way or the other, someday you will die, and someday you will give an account of your choices. If you don't know when you will die, and you are trying to achieve something on your own, there is no guarantee you will get there, and your efforts become meaningless. However, if you subscribe to the belief that there is a God and He does have plans, purposes, and ways greater than our own, it doesn't matter when you die. Your life lives on in the people you have pointed to Jesus. You will never go wrong in looking for God's will for your life, than simply pointing someone to Jesus —not toward fame, stardom, pleasure, indulging in the flesh, gluttony, health, wealth, or anything else, but Jesus. How you communicate that is up to you.

My sister found her way to point people to Jesus through children, through befriending my wife, and through forgiving me. I have found purpose in her death. Many have heard of the Jesus that Hannah served. I have attested to this truth to over a thousand students in the past five years—that I had great loss through the death of my sister but found life right there in the middle of it all. The life I found is the moments. Stop and notice the moments where life is flourishing. Recognize God in the mundane and in the spectacular. If I don't know when I am going to die, then every moment is precious and a gift. James, the half-brother of Jesus, said, "Every good and perfect gift is from above, coming down from the Father of the heavenly lights, who does not change like shifting shadows" (James 1:17).

These moments where I see God work things out is where I find life. As many as the questions of "Why?" are the questions of "What are the chances?" What are the chances I would move when I did because I left a job that I could have easily stayed at or left earlier? I could have never left my hometown at all and not been around to reconcile with Hannah. I could have moved to a different state or country. What are the chances that my time in Colorado was not a waste? We built a relationship with my family in Colorado so that when we had to quickly leave a job, my wife and children were already use to my mom, stepdad, and Annanah.

What are the chances that my job that took us to our apartment was meant to allow me to be free to handle two emotional burdens that semester? The first was Emi's birth, and the second was Hannah's death. What are the chances that less than a month later, I would apply for and get a job up in the northern part of the city, where we wanted to be originally, as a High School Bible teacher at a private Christian school which was where I had originally tried to pursue the previous May?

I had called an old family friend who was the principal this private Christian school asking if there were any openings, and he said they had just filled a Bible position two days before. I felt urged to call him again over Thanksgiving break, two weeks after Hannah died, to ask when the next hiring time was. A Bible position or any position would be a better use of my gifts and talents than the job I had in the computer lab as a glorified tutor. He asked me how I found out there was a job opening, and I was puzzled. "There is a job opening?" He said he'd just had Thanksgiving with our mutual family friends and thought they had told me about the job opening. I said no; I was calling about the next school year. The week before I called him, a teaching position had opened.

When I got to my first interview, I didn't even know what the job was—just that it was to teach the Bible. What are the chances the job I was applying for and that I would eventually get was to teach the part of the Bible I loved the most and had the most training in? The job was to teach the New Testament Epistles to eleventh graders, and at that point, I would have taken on any challenge. If they wanted me to teach kindergartners the book of Numbers, I would have done backflips to connect with them. I would have jumped through any hoop for this job.

God wanted us to be near my sister, near her church, near Mandi who was living down the road in Chandler, and near my parents to walk with them. If you think getting a specific job of teaching the New Testament Epistles to the high-school-student age group I enjoy the most just two weeks after my sister died is chance, then you, my friend, are a believer. That thing you call chance is God, who Paul says is working all things for good, for His good (Romans 8:28). This chance is not random; it has a specific purpose, a specific design. To every "Why did this happen?" question there is an equal "What are the chances of this happening?" These are the connections I made in the weeks and months that followed Hannah's death. This is when death allowed me to see life.

The young-adult-ministries pastor stood up last to speak to the gathering of friends and family who had come to pay their respects to Hannah. I don't remember everything he said. I just know he wore an orange Broncos Jersey and preached the gospel. Our funeral service for Hannah was exactly what we wanted: for Hannah to be remembered and her God to be proclaimed.

16

Raindrops and Teardrops

When the service ended, we moved the casket to the foyer and threw our final Hannah party. Our vision of a duct-taped casket with pens for people to write a parting message came to life. Hannah had tons of different-colored sharpies—two for every color of nail polish she owned and hair dye she had used to color her hair. She would duct-tape every Bible she owned or book she loved. She also loved penguins. Everyone has something they collect, and hers was penguins.

The pattern of duct tape we found was light blue with little cartoon penguins all over it. There was a carefully placed line of duct tape across the highest point of the sides of the wooden casket. If this casket symbolized her story, we were decorating the cover the way she would have wanted. The top was flat; we spread out the multiple colored sharpies and asked friends and family to write on it. It was perfect.

People thought it was weird at first, writing on a casket, but as they saw how excited we were to write on it and invite them over, they realized it was a Hannah thing: duct tape, penguins, and colorful pens. The casket was covered with messages by the time everyone was done. It was a work of art, a masterpiece, something unique that fit her personality to a tee. It was the cover of her final volume, the book with the wooden cover and duct tape keeping it together. My favorite part was writing and reading what people had written. The colorful casket truly represented something that was beautifully mistaken. She shouldn't have had to be in the casket, but we made the celebration of her life beautiful. It was her memory book for the wedding she never had.

You can be broken, shattered, and bruised, and Jesus will tell you to keep walking toward him as He puts the pieces of your life back together. It takes faith to walk and be fixed at the same time, instead of just sitting and waiting. The problem of sitting and waiting is that the pieces that Jesus needs to restore you are not right next to you; they are all sprinkled along a path, a trail that is leading somewhere. As you travel along this trail and pick up these former shades of yourself, Jesus takes them one at a time and begins to mend the broken heart we lost. Your heart can't be fixed in the present location. You can't stay in your guilt, regret, remorse, and anger. You must move toward a goal—a place where there is healing. With every shard of glass restored, the burden of the guilt you carry becomes less, because with each piece of glass Jesus restores, he takes a piece of your guilt with him.

The reality of this journey is that it wasn't only that your heart shattered, it was that something else was put in its place. Where you once found love and compassion, the weight of death fills the void. This calloused heart, this heart of stone, weighs you down. As you begin to allow God to help you walk again—with each passing day, with each interaction with people, with every moment of beauty and memory of the hope lost—Jesus is taking a piece of this hardened heart away and replacing it with a better heart than you had before your loss.

The key, though, is faith. Do you trust that when He is done, you will have a stronger and better heart than the hardened one death brought? It will be better than a heart that has been made stronger at the broken places, better than a heart fixed together with a *kintsugi* gold adhesive. As the prophet Ezekiel declares about the future work of Jesus in his people: "I will give you a new heart and put a new spirit in you; I will remove from you your heart of stone and give you a heart of flesh" (Ezekiel 36:26).

It was at the signing that I found the friends of Hannah I'd been looking for. The two I had prayed to see were sisters. They were the ones who came on our Relient K concert extravaganzas. They used to be in my youth group with Hannah, and now they were as old as Hannah. I hugged them and told them I was sorry for their loss too.

I told them I had been praying for them and that God was never out of their reach. I didn't pry; I just wanted Hannah to be able to pass a message along to them that when their Heavenly Father was ready to see them walking down the road and would run to them. I still pray they find their way back home. My words put tears in their eyes, and then we said our goodbyes. I did what was on my heart and asked if I could pray for them. I hope Hannah's death and the life we brought to her service meant something to them on a level that transcends the mind and goes after the soul.

After this moment of joy, a brief pause in our day of grief and mourning, we had one more thing to do before we completed what we'd set out to do six days earlier. This was going to be the most difficult task of it all. It would be a place of silence, of rain falling as heavy as our tears, the place we didn't want to have to go but was inevitable. We placed Hannah's casket in the hearse and followed it to the cemetery for her final resting place, to lay her in *Sheol*, the grave.

The rain came down steadily when we arrived at the cemetery after the ten-minute drive down the road. I quickly parked, got out, and went to the hearse to carry my sister to where her grave had been dug. H5 had been prepared and was ready for our final goodbye. There was a metal frame over the hole, with straps laid across where they could lower her into the ground. The funeral home had set up a large covering to try to keep us from getting too wet. They had also moved the main flowers from the funeral and placed them around the burial site, and laid turf around the sides of the hole so we didn't have to see it.

The goal of the funeral home, and what they don't tell you, is that seeing the open grave is too difficult. They don't suggest any family stick around for the actual burial. It is better to let the staff do that job alone. Their reasoning is that out of the whole process of what we have had to go through, seeing our loved one lowered into the ground and covered in dirt is an awful sight—an unbearable weight to carry. It's not like what we see in the movies or on tv, where people throw dirt in a whole that the casket is already resting in. So, they cover the hole as best they can so that the last thing we see when we drive away is her casket. If the professional funeral directors who do this for a living told us that we didn't want to see the burial, then we would trust their wisdom. We were hurting already, and it was as if they said, "This is far enough. You have done your part; let us take the rest." They were our Jesus, carrying our cross for us the rest of the way.

I remember that my brother-in-law's father, an older short Egyptian man, appeared to my right, pulling the casket from the hearse through the drizzling rain—no umbrella for the ones who shouldered the task of carrying the casket. I could see the water dripping down his forehead and covering his blazer. The short walk was slow as we traversed the slippery deep grass from the hearse to where the metal altar had been set up for us to place her on. It was this grown man's way, with grown children of his own, of literally carrying our burden with us. He didn't say anything; he just walked with us through the rain and the rain-soaked grass that covered our shoes. The look on his face was cast down with sorrow. This dark-skinned man was my Jesus beside me, carrying the heavy load with me.

The raindrops that had managed to lay atop the casket added texture and movement to the words that had been written on it. I laid my head on top of Hannah's final resting bed, and my hands became soaked as the words bled onto my skin. I kissed her coffin, a long heartfelt goodbye, as my family behind me laid their hands on my back. I wish I could have had several more minutes to myself, but I knew that it wasn't just about me in these moments.

I will never forget the rain that day. The skies spilled out their built-up emotion and matched our tears drop for drop. I would not change the memory of this weather; it complemented our hurt and pain and gave the air a sweet aroma. My family huddled together in the front row of the movable metal awning the cemetery provided. This little cover from the drizzling rain allowed us several minutes to take in the words Hannah's pastor left us with.

This was the moment we needed him the most. None of us could speak or say a word; we needed someone to speak on our behalf. He told us that he had lost his brother some time ago, and it was that experience that allowed him to walk in empathy with us. He shared a verse that reminded us of the power Jesus' words: "In this world, you will have troubles, but take heart! I have overcome the world" (John 16:33b).

He then began to cry as he spoke. I don't remember what he said; I just remember the tears that streamed down his face. He had only known Hannah a little over a year, and he had held his emotions together the whole day. In that moment of saying our final goodbyes, Hannah's pastor began to weep. He wept for his own loss of his brother that was still so fresh in his life, but he also wept for us. I understood why he cried. He too had lost a sibling, and this burial was a reminder of that. He was part of this club that no one chooses to be in, but no one who is in it can leave. We could not have asked for a better pastor to walk with us that day. His heart was opened to us, transparent for us to see.

I thanked him for this. I'm not sure he will ever know the impact his tears had on me. I imagine Jesus was personified in Hannah's pastor in those last words and tears. I imagine Jesus crying with us, knowing the depth of our heartache. The picture of the tattooed, long-bearded man crying over the loss of my sister was another picture of my Jesus who was weeping with me. Hannah's pastor restated these final words: "Jesus has overcome the world."

During the week between the death and the funeral, I had reached out to an old friend. Adam was a student in the youth ministry during my second year of college. His younger brother was one student I had spent the most time with since I started being a youth leader. This student was the one in Hannah's grade. His name was Seth Kahu D'Luzandsky. He was a sophomore when I last saw him standing on the steps of the high school where I picked up my sister and her friend for one of our midnight concert road trips. We made eye contact, and we waved.

Seth had a family trip to ride quads at the sand dunes. I received news the following week that Seth had died that same weekend when his quad collided with a dune buggy. It was a random accident, something that seemed to be avoidable. I was horrified, broken, saddened, and depressed. Seth's older brother, the one I was contacting, was a senior at the time, and seeing his pain mixed with my own was my first taste of death.

When Hannah died, I knew immediately that I wanted to track down Seth's older brother to let him know what had happened. Our parents were good friends back when Hannah and Seth were in grade school. I wanted to let them know about Hannah and ask if they would reach out to my parents, since they were veteran grievers of a lost child. I also wanted to know if I could ask him for advice. Seth's older brother was only a few years younger than me, but it had been almost nine years since Seth died. I knew Seth's death had taken an emotional toll on both myself and Hannah as well. It was a burden I carried for a while. It was possibly how God humbled me and prepared me for Hannah.

When teenagers grieve, it is like a forest set ablaze. Teenagers do not handle death very well. Or possibly, they are more real than adults, who bottle it up. Something in my heart told me to reach out to Seth's older brother, even though we had not spoken in years. He replied to me the following week of Thanksgiving. These words have stuck with me to this day.

Facebook Message on November 26, 2013:

Even though it'll be nine years since Seth's death this coming February, I definitely still miss him. The frequency has changed over the years, but I especially miss him during moments like this week where family togetherness is a major focus for most people.

Even though I miss him, when he does come up in my thoughts, or actually more when he comes up in conversation, I find it has become an opportunity to reflect on God's provision in my life and my parents' lives. While we take comfort in the fact that Seth is with God, we're still heartbroken that he's not with us. God, however, has still used Seth's absence for His glory, even though small things like people getting the chance to hear that we haven't abandoned God in our sadness. I certainly asked myself whether God was still real, especially in the first days and weeks after Seth's death. I eventually decided that all that I'd come to know see, and trust about God was still true, even though I didn't understand why God let Seth die. I still don't know why Seth had to die. But I've eventually been able to receive peace that my not knowing why he died still doesn't invalidate everything else. That's one of the hardest things for me to accept about my Christian faith.

I've experienced a version of what you are going through, and it's awful. I found that sometimes the loneliest moments came months after Seth died and I had returned to my "normal" routine. While surviving family members like us wish God gave us answers, He only promises to give us His presence.

—Adam D'Luzandsky

His words were exactly what I needed to hear: validation, comfort, hope, experience, and direction. Not abandoning God in our sadness was the first piece of advice I took to heart; the second was the admission that he did not know why God allowed Seth to die, but that did not negate everything else about God he believed to be true. Just because we face pain doesn't mean we have to throw what we believe to be true about God out the window.

Adam used some carefully chosen words that brought me to a deeper realization of my new reality. He said, "Surviving family members like us." Hannah is survived by her four older siblings, her parents and now, many babies later, thirteen nieces and nephews. I am a survivor.

Through Adam, I learned about God's promised presence. When forced into the presence of death, it is God's presence that we search for, long for, hope for, and find our healing in. "Be content with what you have, because God has said, 'Never will I leave you; never will I forsake you'" (Hebrews 13:5). Being content is being at peace, even when you experience a death and your life is thrown into the chaos of the unknown. The tether in our storms is the truth that God has promised to never leave or forsake his people. God is a good God, and I do not understand his ways. As Paul wrote, "Who has known the mind of the Lord?" (Romans 11:34a). I trust that he is a good God, and nothing can separate me from his love.

Paul ends his description of all that God has done for us through Christ with a list of things that cannot separate us from God. The first statement is this: "For I am convinced that neither death nor life ..." (Romans 8:38a). I always assumed it only meant *my* death and life, but I think it is much broader. Our life and the living we walk among and our death or loved ones who have died in our midst cannot or will not separate us from Christ.

I can't fix myself. I can't fix my parents. But I know of a man who suffered and is able to empathize with our human weakness. God sent Jesus to taste death for us all, as the author of Hebrews states (Hebrews 2:9). Death is not unknown to God and is not the end for those who have called upon the name of Jesus. My sister believed this wholeheartedly.

If you have lost someone, I am so sorry for your loss. If you know of someone who has lost someone, just be present. Be Jesus to them. Walk beside them and talk if needed, or just be okay with silence. Everyone grieves differently.

If you haven't experienced death, you will, and I pray this book prepares you for that time. Death waits for no one, but God's timing is perfect. So, do you trust Him? The only way to solidify your faith is to decide now how you will respond before the storm comes. Decide now: even if God allows the worst to happen, will you still trust that he is a good God, and will you follow him through the unknown? If you say, "I will follow, but ...," you are placing a border of where you are unwilling to go either physically or emotionally. You must decide today that no matter the pain that is to be experienced in this life, no matter who you lose or what you lose, you will follow Jesus in faith.

If you wait until tragedy strikes, your faith will be limited, and you will struggle to see anything past the approaching wave. Let us fix "our eyes on Jesus," the author "and perfecter of faith" (Hebrews 12:2). Choose now to keep your eyes on Jesus and not the pain that is to come. Don't fear it. Don't dwell on it. Just trust. May you see that even in death, God will allow you to see life for what it truly is: precious, fragile and meaningful.

17

The Last Day of Regret

A student once said to me, after I had shared my story of Hannah and her Borderline Personality Disorder, "It is hard to differentiate between the person God makes one to be and the mental disorder." Looking back at my tumultuous relationship with Hannah, I realized that she and I were both somewhat crazy. I was OCD, and she was borderline. My student was right and spoke so much truth in that moment—that I had a hard time seeing Hannah as the person God made or Hannah the one struggling with a disorder.

Several years after Hannah's passing, I was put into proximity with another person who had BPD. I didn't know it at the time, but I had all these feelings of anger and frustration and would tell Katie, "This is exactly how I felt around Hannah." I could not figure it out. Was I the common denominator? Was I the problem?

Thankfully, God placed in my life a friend who was working at an adult mental institution. He told me that the patients who caused him the biggest issues were the ones who had BPD. He began to ask me questions about this person and our interactions, and I felt like he had been watching us. My jaw dropped. I was dumbfounded.

"How do you know all these problems that have occurred? How have you predicted all of this person's behavior?"

My friend described in detail what people with BPD are like and why they respond to things the way they do. Every similarity between the person I was currently having a conflict with and Hannah suddenly made sense. I could finally look back and predict or find the pattern of Hannah's behavior—why she said and did the things she did.

A lot of my guilt subsided in the following weeks as I read the recommended BPD book, *Stop Walking on Eggshells*. Where I had brushed BPD off to my mom back in Colorado as not a big deal, I finally realized how great of a deal it was. I had not been approaching Hannah as someone who could not see the world around her normally. When I said Hannah was selfish, she was, because that is a strong part of the disorder. When Hannah would bring the conversation back to her, I felt like she did it on purpose, and she *was*. That is a strong part of BPD. All the things that bothered me in Colorado could be traced back to me not understanding her disorder and expecting her to behave normally. She couldn't; it was not possible, given where she was at in dealing with her own disorder.

Do I regret not understanding this? Sure. But I no longer carry the guilt that I was to blame for her sadness or brokenness.

After four months of waiting, the autopsy report from the medical examiner revealed that Hannah had several drugs in her system. Based on the lack of evidence of a suicide—mainly a missing note of intent, a "suicide letter," and the texts with her friends regarding her desire to try again—the investigation was ruled inconclusive. There was no proof of foul play. She simply made a bad judgment. After she ingested the codeine, which woke her up and kept her awake, she tried to medicate herself back to sleep. She had two other drugs in her toxic screening report: one was a generic sleeping pill she kept in her room and the other was the general ingredients for Nyquil, which has alcohol and acetaminophen in it.

Hannah took a lot of an upper, codeine. It was a more condensed and potent prescription than she was used to, and it was meant to be taken in small doses. Mixing that with sleeping pills and NyQuil, she created a deadly cocktail. Her death was an accidental suicide. She simply misjudged how many things she could put into her system.

Not that it brings her back but knowing that her intent was not to take her own life did bring us some peace. In a world where suicide seems to be an answer, the person who commits it will never know its devastating consequences. Hannah, however, was a fighter up to the end. I know she had suicidal thoughts at various times, which Hannah handled by cutting herself and self-medicating. My mom recalled so many times in Colorado when Hannah could have just as easily died. If she had died then, it would have been when she was at her lowest point in life. Instead, God allowed her to pass when she was finally improving and becoming better.

One relapse does not define you. However, know about the interactions of the medications you are taking. It is a matter of life and death. What seemed like a small lack in judgment turned out to have deadly consequences, but no one is to blame. The surviving family members accept what happened, and Hannah is finally at rest from all her trials and tribulations of this life. "Then I heard a voice from heaven say, 'Write this: Blessed are the dead who die in the Lord from now on.' 'Yes,' says the Spirit, 'they will rest from their labor, for their deeds will follow them' (Revelation 14:13).

God has a plan. He knows every hair on our head (Luke 12:7) and sees where any and all paths can lead, and we need to trust him with each step. If your heart's position toward God is to pursue him and do good because he died for you, then you will never stray far from him. Even when you do stray, there is always a way back.

My sister found her way back in the end. She was the prodigal daughter, and I am grateful she died among friends who loved her, at a church that supported her, and with a purpose she had been looking for. The day she died was her last day of regretting all her life's choices, because now she is with Jesus. The one who has put the final piece of her broken heart together removed her heart of stone and has met her at the end of the trail of shattered glass.

It turns out that these were never Hannah's volumes to begin with. She was never meant to have section H5 in adult nonfiction; it was not how the library was designed. These volumes were my own, and her life has been interwoven into the volumes of those that have survived her. It seems that those who die unexpectedly were never meant to have their own place in heaven's library but were merely here for a short time to impact the lives of those around them. Hannah's story is an intimate part of my own, section M4, as she will be in the lives of those closest to her: my wife, Katie; my children, Kyle, Levi, Emalynn, and Lillian; my mom and stepdad; my brother; and my two remaining sisters and all of their children. It would be presumptuous to assume that we all will have our own volumes. My volumes, which include Hannah's, could end abruptly. The writing could stop, and you would find out that I was merely here to be a part of your story.

The point is this: those who leave this life early always leave the rest of us wondering, "Why did they die so soon?" The answer is that their life was never meant to be its own set of volumes but to be a part of ours. If you have lost a friend or family member to an unexpected death, their story didn't change; that was their story all along. It is not their story that changed, it is your story that is supposed to change because of them.

I said to one of the twins the week after Hannah's passing, "There is a reason God allowed Hannah to die and has left the four of us here. We are supposed to do something or quite possibly *be* something greater because of her." In that moment, I was reminded that life is a challenge. We are given an opportunity to do something for evil or for good. The challenge to do something good can cause some people to never pursue their God-given design. As Christians, we have something that empowers us to accomplish this good: The Holy Spirit.

The Holy Spirit illuminates the world we live in and allows us to become the person God designed us to be. We cannot fear the light in us that God wants to use to do great things. It is a city on a hill that becomes brighter as the night gets darker.

Our real question about death is not "Why did they die?" but "Why am I still here?" The answer to that question is possibly one of our greatest fears. Is it possible that God has something greater for my life? Am I set apart for something much more extraordinary that has only been made possible by having known the ones I have lost unexpectedly? There is a reason God has left me here and a reason God placed Hannah in my life for twenty-four years. Is it to bring others hope? Is it to walk with those who have experienced a loss? Is it to record in stone the events of the loved one who passed so the story cannot be forgotten or lost? Yes to it all.

I gladly carry this responsibility to share my sister's story. I am humbled to admit my failures, because they are what make me human. We all mess up in our relationships. Our family of origin can be the most difficult to reconcile with. I pray my honesty allows someone to realize which person in the story they are and can extend grace or gain wisdom from someone who has done and said things wrong or right. We need to give more grace to ourselves, to our friends, to our siblings, to our parents, and to our children. Maybe we can be the first to be humbled before our family and take the higher road and love even if it hurts.

I struggle to find an answer for my parents who have lost their child. I struggle to find an answer for my stepdad who has lost his only child. My heart crumbles in fear at the thought of the inner turmoil he must have gone through and is still going through. The memory of the tears he cried with me that week—the strongest man in the world weeping and looking utterly lost—will be a reminder that even grown men break down and cry when faced with loss. The answer I have given to us all does not seem to compute for a father who has lost his only child. For him to ask "Why am I still here?" in his old age does not make sense.

He is too old to have more children. He was supposed to outlive her and didn't. He will have to come to the realization that God is still using him even though the person he spent the past twenty-four years growing, nurturing, and pruning to life is gone. It will take years—no, it will take the rest of his life and my mother's life—to grieve and come to terms with their loss. That is why their grief goes unanswered here. I cannot speak for them, and I have come to realize I cannot carry my parents' burden. They don't expect me to, and I don't think I am meant to.

It is the parental figures who take the brunt of the pain when someone has passed away suddenly at a young age. When parents lose a child, they lose their dream. When children grow up, they leave their mother and father and eventually take on the role of being an adult, either through starting a family or pursuing a career. This is a natural cycle. Eventually, we will all lose our parents, and all our parents pray we will outlive them. For a parent who loses a child, there is a permanent hole that will never be filled.

My prayer for my parents has always been that no matter how much pain they are in, no matter how big the void feels, they will face it together and not push the other one away. If I were to offer hope to grieving parents, it could only be validation. Your pain is great. Your pain is real. Your child's life was precious, and I'm so sorry for your loss. I'm sorry for your lost dream, your lost hope, and your lost love.

Maybe that's what grieving parents need? They need to know that we have not forgotten about their child. While they are still reliving the loss daily, they want everyone who has moved on to not forget about the one who is gone. I bet if you asked these parents, they would want to sit down and talk about their child with you. Maybe spend some time walking around a cemetery, carry some flowers, and look for a couple standing next to a grave. Ask them about their story.

I've learned not to be afraid to talk about those who have died. It might seem taboo, but talking to parents about the child they lost, for some, can be soothing for their soul. There will be tears, but they are good tears. These parents might not even know they need to talk about their child or that they *can* talk about their child. I've learned to just ask, "Can I hear more about all of your children?" You might be surprised at the response you get.

As stated earlier, the last step in becoming an adult is seeing your parents fail. Until we realize the imperfection of our role models, we idolize them, and we are living in a state of immaturity. Our thoughts about the world are that our parents will always protect us or be there for us. When we become adults, we see their imperfections and realize it isn't fair to idolize them. Yes, we respect them and learn from them, but the reality of our world is that we have become one of them, and they have been one of us the whole time. Imperfect!

Hannah's volumes are a part of mine now. Once I realized this, I had to change. There is something Hannah has taught me that I can't ignore. God gave Hannah twenty-four years to teach me something, and it would be a shame to miss it. Some people might think it is arrogant of me to assume Hannah's life was only meant to teach me a lesson—that it wasn't for her own enjoyment or satisfaction. I would argue that Hannah is okay with that. If she knew she had little time left on this earth, she would want my life to be better without her, not less because she was gone.

God gave me Hannah, and she left me better than when she found me. All the pain in my life up until the day she died was released in the car that day I drove to the ER. In the flashes of my memory, I saw her pain and transformation. I saw that God was preparing me to experience a miraculous change inside of me. I would be different after having gone through this death. I would have walked through the veil that separates the living from the dead and find Jesus standing there waiting to show me the bigger plans he has for me.

My sister's death was not in vain or without purpose. As Hannah understood that she was broken but could still be used, I have fully embraced that same awareness. I'm broken, but I'm okay. I will serve my God no matter the cost.

I think I was finally able to give Hannah that final send-off with the validation she had been longing for that Halloween at our apartment. In our walk around the apartment while trick-or-treating with my boys, she started talking to me about her ministry at Cornerstone. She talked about her babysitting jobs on the side and that she was able to earn money. I listened and had a pleasant conversation that evening. Simply telling her I was proud of her and that I loved her fixed, in some way, years of silence between us. Even though I grumbled about having to include her in conversations the weeks leading up to that night, I think God spared me more pain by allowing me to affirm her an encourage her. My last conversation is not something I regret but memorialize within my heart and mind.

It all comes down to this: was Hannah's death her last day of regret, overdosing on medication? Was it my last day of not having to regret knowing that I had left her with peace intact? Is there ever a last day we regret our choices? The answer I have come to is no. There will never be a last day of regret, because regret isn't the problem. We confuse regret and guilt. We use these words synonymously in our English language, but this fails us.

One therapist told me that I live in the world of "should and should not." I always beat myself up, making statements of imperatives, personally placed rules, and expectations that no one else has for me. These are statements of guilt. Instead, I need to make statements of preference: "It would have been nice to do this, but I didn't get to it." Or "I would have preferred to have said this, but I can change it next time."

Regret is a statement of preference. It is amoral, meaning it is not right or wrong. I would have preferred to have responded to Hannah differently in Colorado. I think she could have heard me better.

The hurtful option, the thing that brings you down, is guilt. Guilt is very different from regret. Guilt is taking the blame for something you cannot control. Guilt is thinking that you could have done something to prevent a tragedy—that you are to blame. Guilt is placing yourself in the position of God, thinking you can control, stop, or allow things. God would ask of us as he did of his servant Job:

> Then the Lord spoke to Job out of the storm, "Brace yourself like a man; I will question you, and you shall answer me. Would you discredit my justice? Would you condemn me to justify yourself? Do you have an arm like God's, and can your voice thunder like his?" (Job 40:6-9).

After Job had lost everything and everyone, he began to ask God why this had happened, and God finally spoke to him. Some people interpret this section to mean you are not allowed to question God's sovereignty. I think it's telling us that we actually can question God like Job, and he will respond, he will speak; he will not remain silent when we confront Him.

The problem to fix is to not carry the guilt. Job thinks he has done something to cause all his calamity, but God points out to Job that the burden of pain is not his to carry. Are you as strong as God? Then don't try to carry something God has intended to carry for you.

Guilt is also unforgiveness toward yourself. When we don't forgive ourselves, we are not accepting God's forgiveness of us. If God forgives all our transgressions, removes all our iniquities, and purifies us to the point of his presence forever residing in us through the Holy Spirit, then not forgiving ourselves is telling God his forgiveness is not enough. Guilt will prevent you from reaching true peace that can only come from accepting that God has forgiven you, and therefore you need to extend that same grace and forgive yourself.

Jesus says you must love your neighbor as yourself. Do you love yourself? There may not be an end to regret, but guilt will only have its moment in the sun if you let it. There is a higher power that has provided a way to absolve you of all sin, mistakes, failures, and brokenness on this side of eternity to prepare you for the other side.

When I meet Hannah on the other side, I will be guilt-free and shame free, and my regret will be whisked away in an instant because our relationship will be made perfect. All the preferences of how I would like to have treated her will be accomplished on that great and glorious day of the coming of our Lord Jesus. I never longed for heaven until someone I loved was there. Not that I'm done with where I am at, but I have a sister waiting for me next to Jesus, and my regret will simply cease to exist, because our perfection in Jesus will allow us to forever be reconciled for eternity. The regret will be fixed, because I will be able to tell Hannah all the things I would have preferred to say if she were still with me today.

Maybe I won't need to say anything at all. Maybe we will just know and embrace, and all our pain and tears will be wiped away. For now, I will wait with all the other saints before me for that Day. "He who testifies to these things says, 'Yes, I am coming soon.' Amen. Come, Lord Jesus" (Revelation 22:20).

Epilogue

The house on Jacob Avenue was once again preparing us to live with my parents. A couple of years after Hannah's passing, our lives were beginning to settle with new jobs and new houses, and then God brought us to another change. When my parents moved from the Jacob Avenue house, they were heartbroken, because that was the house that held their last memories of their daughter.

Selling a house and moving is a difficult chapter to endure in the process of mourning loved ones. It is hard to accept change, because it seems as if one is forced to say goodbye to the visual memories that we hold on to. It was Hannah's last house, last room, last pool that she swam in, last home to be with her parents in.

Life moves on after someone dies, but for those standing next to the dead, change is painful and often unwanted. I know there are people who want to run away from their pain, but when a parent loses a child, I think most fall into the category of wishing for everything to stay the same. Parents wish people could understand their desire not to have their child forgotten, because their child was their life and still is their life. The child's death is not the end for the parents; in fact, it's a new beginning that is marked by suffering. Somehow, people can move on and hold on. It's both: you must come to accept the death and yet have very concrete memories to take with you along the way.

When my stepdad was thinking of retirement, after they had already left the Jacob Avenue house, we were living within a block from them. We didn't have a pool, so we spent our summer days there.

I jokingly said to my mom one day, "We should sell both our houses and go in on one big one." My mom laughed it off.

Several months later, when my dad was counting the year and a half left of working, he had to decide about retirement. My parents realized they could not keep living in their house. Retirement could only afford them a two-bedroom home, and honestly, it was all they needed. However, my mom's deep desire to host Christmas and other family events where she could see her grandchildren would be crushed by the reality of a smaller living space. My stepdad approached me and said, "Your mother and I wanted to know if you were serious about buying a house together and living together."

I immediately thought to myself, *yes, having a larger house is always better if we can afford it.* I told him yes, but I needed to see how seriously Katie had considered it, because I was joking when we first made the comment. When Katie and I talked, there was no issue or need for discussion. Katie was prepared and ready to live with and get along with my mom and stepdad. Stone Fence Drive and Jacob Avenue were not wasted life tragedies, missed opportunities, or wrong directions in my journey to find God's calling. They were moments of preparation, of fostering a healthy relationship to make our new living arrangement work.

I think Hannah would be happy to know that Katie and I are taking care of her mom and dad. As much as we worried about her, and as much as Hannah cared for me, Hannah cared about my parents the most. Hannah cared about the things they did, cried when they did, was happy when they were happy, and was mad when they were mad. Her empathy toward them was a defining point of her life.

I never would have guessed that part of my calling would be to take care of my mom and stepdad and watch over them as a testament to Hannah's life and legacy. Her legacy is in me, the prodigal brother, no different from his sister, humbled by how delicate life is. Thank you for teaching this to me, my Hannah. I can see you now, and I know I will see you again.